Natural Horsemanship

Natural Horsemanship

Based on a
Passionate Riding Instructor's Papers:
With An Appendix by Paul Plinzner

By Otto de la Croix

An English translation
*Natürliche Reitkunst nach Papieren eines
passionierten Reitlehrers*
second edition from 1905
by Richard F. Williams

Title: *Natural Horsemanship Based on a Passionate Riding Instructor's Papers: With An Appendix by Paul Plinzner*

Author: Otto de la Croix

An English translation of *Natürliche Reitkunst nach Papieren eines passionierten Reitlehrers* by Richard F. Williams

Copyright 2026 Richard F. Williams, All rights reserved

ISBN: 9781948717762

All rights reserved. No part of this publication may be reproduced, distributed, or transmitted in any form or by any means, including photocopying, recording, or other electronic or mechanical methods, without the prior written permission of the publisher, except in the case of brief quotations embodied in critical reviews and certain other noncommercial uses permitted by copyright law.

Any use of this publication to train generative artificial intelligence ("AI") technologies is expressly prohibited. The author and publisher reserve all rights to license uses of this work for generative AI training and development of machine learning language models.

Readers should always ensure that the appropriate safety equipment is worn: riding boots, gloves and, if necessary, a body protector. The publisher also recommends a correctly fitted hard hat to a minimum of EN1384/BSEN1384 or PAS015 standard.

Cover and Interior design: Robert Ashbaugh

Originally published in German:
Natürliche Reitkunst nach Papieren eines passionierten Reitlehrers, 2nd edition, Berlin 1905, Ernst Siegfried Mittler & Sohn.

All rights reserved under the law of June 19, 1901.

Published by Xenophon Press LLC

7518 Bayside Road, Franktown, Virginia 23354-2106, U.S.A.

XenophonPress@gmail.com

www.XenophonPress.com

Publisher's Introduction

Few periods in the history of horsemanship have generated as much serious disagreement as the one from which this book comes. Around the turn of the twentieth century, the riding world was no longer divided merely by matters of taste or national style, but by fundamentally different ideas about how a horse should be trained, balanced, and understood.

At the center of this divide stood two figures whose names still provoke discussion today: James Fillis and Paul Plinzner.

To a modern reader, the disagreement is often reduced to outward appearance—high carriage versus deeper flexion, elevation versus compression, brilliance versus submission. But that framing misses the point. What was really being argued was causality: whether correct posture could be created directly through the hand and rein, or whether it could only arise as a consequence of correct balance, engagement, and impulsion initiated from the rider's seat.

The Fillis tradition, admired by many for its refinement and spectacular results, placed primary emphasis on the forehand. Elevation, collection, and expression were sought through careful management of the neck and poll by a powerful, educated hand. For its proponents, the visible result justified the method. If the horse moved brilliantly and obediently, the system was deemed successful. Yet even at the time, critics questioned whether such results represented genuine self-carriage—or only its appearance.

Paul Plinzner's position stood in direct opposition to this logic. He did not merely disagree with particular techniques; he rejected the idea of riding from front to back altogether. In his view, all true collection must originate behind the saddle, through the engagement and stepping-under of the hindquarters and the activation of an elastic, working back. The forehand could not be shaped independently without falsifying the result. Contact, flexion, and elevation were not objectives to be imposed, but effects that necessarily followed correct work from behind.

These ideas were not debated calmly. The equestrian world of the period polarized around them. Riders became "Fillis men" or "Plinzner men," as if allegiance to a name could replace careful analysis. Methods hardened into identities. In the noise of controversy, the horse itself often disappeared from view.

Natural Horsemanship Based on a Passionate Riding Instructor's Papers enters this conversation in a different way. It is not a manifesto, and it is not an attack. Rather than defending Plinzner by authority or dismissing Fillis by caricature, the author proceeds more patiently—and more rigorously. He follows the rider's aids through the horse's body step by step and asks a simple but demanding question: if balance, anatomy, and natural laws are taken seriously, what must follow?

The book does not begin with doctrine. It begins with balance—literal, physical balance—and traces how every genuine improvement in posture, gait, and responsiveness arises from it. Again and again, the reader is shown that when the rider's seat activates the hindquarters correctly, the horse responds by rounding the back, seeking contact, and organizing the forehand. When the forehand is manipulated in isolation, the result may look convincing, but the internal connections are broken, and the cost is borne by the horse.

Read this way, the Fillis–Plinzner contrast stops being a matter of schools and becomes a matter of testing ideas against reality. The author is not interested in which system produces the most impressive picture. He is interested in which one holds up when subjected to the horse's actual structure and movement. The question he returns to repeatedly is an uncompromising one: *what happens in the horse's body when we do this?*

Modern readers will likely be struck by how familiar this debate sounds. Contemporary discussions of biomechanics, back activity, self-carriage, and welfare echo these pages closely. What is often presented today as recent discovery was already clearly understood—if not universally accepted—more than a century ago.

One of the most unusual features of this work lies not only in what it argues, but in how it is presented. Names are minimized. Authority is withheld. The reader is asked to judge the argument on coherence and consequence rather than reputation. Only at the end does the author reveal that the editor, the author, and the original publisher of the 1905 edition were all the same person.

This was no accident. It reflects the book's underlying philosophy. Just as true collection cannot be imposed from the hand, true understanding cannot rest on borrowed prestige. The ideas must stand on their own.

To help place this work more fully in its historical context, Xenophon Press has included Appendix A: "Are Modifications in the Training of the Soldier's Horse Necessitated by the Increased Demands Placed upon the Cavalry?" (1886) by Paul Plinzner, originally published in the German "Militär-Wochenblatt." This first-ever complete English translation makes this pivotal part of the discussion readily available to our readers. It was not included, but often referred to in de la Croix' 1905 work. Another article, "The Plinzner System and Cavalry Riding" (1900), also published in the "Militär-Wochenblatt," presents an anonymous reaction to Plinzner's proposals directly and without mediation. Read alongside the main text, these two pieces allow the reader to engage with the ideas that shaped this period first hand.

Readers encountering frequent references to James Fillis should also know that his principal work, *Principles of Dressage and Equitation—also known as Breaking and Riding, with military commentaries*—is widely available in a modern English edition from Xenophon Press. Consulting that volume provides essential context for understanding the position this book examines and critiques.

This edition is offered not as a historical curiosity, but as a serious contribution to a discussion that is still very much alive. For anyone who has ever wondered whether correct riding begins in the hand or in the seat, whether balance precedes form or follows it, this book offers not slogans, but carefully reasoned answers—drawn from observation, logic, and sustained attention to the horse.

— Richard F. Williams
Publisher and Translator

Foreword by the Editor (to the first edition)

The moment is rarely favorable to sharply re-examine the truly natural foundations of horsemanship.

Almost simultaneously, we see emerge: on the one hand, the deep-flexion method of the Paul Plinzner system; on the other, the high head carriage of the James Fillis phenomenon—and between the two stands the equestrian world, perplexed: who is right?

If the foundations on which the common understanding rests were firm and complete, its conclusions well thought out and convincing, its line of reasoning coherent and thorough, then it would be easy to dismiss one or the other of the new systems.

The official riding instruction has long been ridiculed by many—unjustly! It remains, for the military, the best that we have. If more capable riders on better horses than those owned by the army achieve faster progress by other methods, that only proves that the instruction manual has the invaluable advantage of respecting terrain limitations and the right rhythm of what is realistically achievable.

It does, however, have one flaw—albeit an innocent one: concepts that were developed after it, particularly the idea of "hindquarter engagement," are naturally foreign to it. The fact that it still embodies the essence of that concept is not recognized by the majority. Thus, it easily gives the impression of being outdated and obsolete.

I have found its principles—admittedly enhanced by one factor that had previously been consistently neglected, namely "the natural crookedness of the horse"—in *the papers of a passionate riding instructor*, essentially modernized.

I tested them over the years in this new guise and found one great advantage: they are easy to understand. Especially for the common man! The practical outcome was that a better-suited recruit, after only 14 days, and the average one after 3 to 4 weeks, began not just mounting but truly shaping his horse.

Therefore, I believe in their persuasive power, even for wider audiences—even if the main practical proof on the horse itself is missing here. Reserving the right to highlight key points in individual chapters through annotations or a brief concluding word, I now let the "passionate riding instructor" speak for himself.

One final remark may be allowed. It concerns anonymity. Until now, outstanding individuals have dominated the arena through their accomplishments. And the result? The present day's unconvincing battle cry: "The Plinzners, the Fillis followers!"—Let us, for once, let the matter speak for itself! Let us present arguments, and also demand counterarguments! Let the individual be left completely out of it—as an experiment!

Foreword to the Second [1905] Edition

The kind reception that *Natural Horsemanship* has received from both the riding public and the critics could only serve as encouragement to perfect the second edition as much as possible. Numerous passages have therefore been revised, partly to increase formal clarity, partly to eliminate factual ambiguities.

May the book, even in this new form, find friends! Above all, may the essential goal of this work—to once again demonstrate, in contrast to other trends, that the principles of the official riding instruction are the only true and unshakable ones, precisely because they are natural—be achieved for every reader.

-Editor of the Second Edition
Berlin, 1905

Table of Contents

Publisher's Introduction	v
Foreword by the Editor (to the First Edition)	vii
Foreword to the Second (1905) Edition	viii
Chapter One: The Artificial and Natural Foundations of Campaign Riding (field riding)	1
Chapter Two: The Back and Its Importance for the Horse's Gaits	15
Chapter Three: The Rider's Aids and their Relationship to the Horse's Movement	25
Chapter Four: On Collection, and the Rider's Aids for Achieving It	48
Chapter Five: Purpose and Importance of the Lateral Movements in Dressage. How They are to be Executed. Conclusions for the Training	63
Chapter Six: The Hard and the Soft Side of the Horse	85
Chapter Seven: About the Rider's Aids on the "Bent" or Crooked Horse	94
Chapter Eight: The Plinzner system — Fillis — *Natural Horsemanship*	107
Appendix A: *"Are modifications in the training of the soldier's horse necessitated by the increased demands placed upon the cavalry?"* By Paul Plinzner	136
From "Militär-Wochenblatt" No. 6, 7 August 1886 [Military Riding Gazette]	
Publisher's Afterword	143
Xenophon Press Library	145

Chapter One
The Artificial and Natural Foundations of Campaign Riding (field riding)

From many recent writings and articles in journals about campaign riding—we mention: v. Rosenberg, *Zusammengewürfelte Gedanken über unseren Dienst* [Collected Thoughts on Our Service], von Holleuffer's Werk work on pillar work [*Die Bearbeitung des Reit- und Kutschpferdes zwischen den Pilaren*] (The training of the riding and carriage horse between the pillars), Count von Geldern, *Das Gewicht in der Rampagnereiterei* [The Role of Weight inCampaign Riding], and Stall Master, [Paul] Plinzner's widely noted article[1] in the "Military Riding Gazette" from August 7, 1886—it becomes apparent that their authors, champions of art, differ in certain points from the currently prevailing theory.

What these positions have in common, in our view, is the endeavor to gain new insights into the influence of rein and seat aids and their relationship to the horse's movement. This is, of course, never stated outright, but when here the unity of aids is declared the main goal, and their "weight" is proclaimed as the most essential factor in controlling the horse, then there is at least an indirect contradiction to the conception that finds the essence of riding in rein and head work and in establishing a formal posture.

Whoever has studied the theory will certainly find that none of this is its fundamental intention. But as an honest person, one must admit that in many places, it seems as though it were.

And if one even ventures into practice to observe the actual effectiveness of the theory in place, one will hear much about rein and seat positions, about hand and weight aids, and so little about leg aids that one must recognize the necessity of a sharper clarification by the theorists themselves. We believe we understand the reasons behind the inconsistencies of current theory.

It is presently in a transitional state. It has adopted a new principle—the work "from back to front"—without discarding everything handed down from its predecessors. But such a discard is necessary because the new system runs directly counter to the old: new wine in old skins never turns out well.

As things currently stand, the theory is based on two foundations: one traditional, inherited from classical school riding; the other natural, grounded in self-evident principles derived from the simplest laws of nature and the obvious experiences of practical riding.

The gospel of the former is: rein and posture, hand work. The gospel of the latter: development of the strength of the hindquarters and forehand.

---

[1] *The first edition of chapter one was already written in 1886, before the publication of the works by Plinzner and Fillis. The entire conceptual thread developed and substantiated therein still holds relevance today. [See Appendix A for Plinzner's article.] - The Editor.*

The Artificial and Natural Foundations

Where there is tradition, there is always misunderstanding—and so it is here! The classical school riding placed its full emphasis on rein and head carriage as the highest value! It worked with means we no longer possess, toward goals we no longer pursue!

The riders were different! There were no exceptions. The horse was a means of transportation; they rode, mostly by necessity. The dressage masters were also different! The noblemen had their stable masters, whose life's work was the training of the horse! Dressage itself had a different nature! There were no divisions by age or purpose—ten to twelve horses, often ridden by fairly unskilled riders; each horse was individually brought to a certain degree of skill by the stable master. The purpose was different! The horse was not merely to show some degree of collection or sure-footedness over terrain—it was to demonstrate grace, polished demeanor, and poise at festivals and ceremonial displays.

The dressage methods were different: longeing, pillar work were not passed onto the young nobleman himself but prepared for him with elevated effort. In this situation, horses that moved independently of the reins, purely on their legs, and *balanced the rider's weight*[2] without relying on the mouth were virtually indispensable! It was, in a sense, self-evident!

The ambition, the striving to create something truly noble and complete, found its expression in pure, swinging gaits with a steady, refined contact. This was contrary to the usual, utilitarian manner—the way the so-called "school horse," worked solely for utility, was managed.

One had to invent something new—and so invented the lateral movements, the airs above the ground, and demanded rein and hand work down to the smallest details; so much so that even during the school jumps, flexion and rein aids were expected.

When the old school riders bent, turned, and led their horses through lateral movements and similar efforts, these horses often bore the weight behind the vertical. In other words, it was about a product that went far beyond utilitarian needs.

They intentionally made the art of riding more difficult: only those capable of managing the more refined work were to be called "masters."

But when this work is transferred to average riders and average horses, we know where it leads; for the period of backward working—from front to back—in which all natural impulsion was lost to endless rein and hand work, has already been assessed.

Preserving remnants from this period could only be justified if the new principle—working from back to front—did not, in fact, account for everything we demand today in terms of rein and head positioning from our horses.

---

[2] *"Balanced the rider's weight"—i.e., without relying on rein contact for balance.*

Let us examine this in particular as we now turn our attention to the natural foundation of campaign riding.

We call it "natural" because its principles arise directly from general laws of nature, from everyday experiences that are easily observable by anyone, and from the natural construction of the horse.

The laws of nature that now come into discussion are, above all, the simple conditions for balance:

I. Like every other moving body, a horse under a rider will only move calmly and in balance ("in equilibrium"[3]) when:
1. The center of gravity remains in the horse's natural position and, apart from the inherent adjustments caused by movement, is not otherwise altered;
2. The limbs (legs) move and land evenly;
3. The horse is not driven away by pain, restlessness, or any similar disturbance caused externally.

These laws apply universally—from the most poorly trained horse to the most highly refined one, from the freshest beginner to the most advanced dressage horse.

II. Changes in the center of gravity of such a moving body, provided they are neither too abrupt nor too extreme—so that the limbs can adapt calmly—will alter the movement, slow it down, deflect it to the right or left, without disturbing the balance.

From this, the natural rider concludes:

I. Neck and head, when calmly carried in the same place, have little to do with forward movement. These parts are not levers that act on the horse, but rather act like the rudder[4] on a ship, guiding the motion of the whole mass.

The equestrian term "balance," which denotes the state in which the horse bears weight evenly between forehand and hindquarters, must not be confused here. What we mean is purely the physical property that applies to any moving body—including, for example, a horse moving heavily on the forehand.

The reins act like a rudder extending forward, which precisely follows the movement of the torso and the muscular exertion of the legs, just as the rudder follows the course of a ship.

However, this only holds true under the condition that the horse remains in balance on all four legs—and does not, for example, have the weight of its torso carried by the reins.

---

[3] *The "equestrian" concept of balance introduced by Seidler, which designates the condition of the horse in which the forehand and hindquarters are evenly loaded, is not to be understood here: rather, we mean only the purely physical property that belongs to any moving body—for example, also to the horse that is moving entirely on the forehand.*
[4] *"Rudder"—metaphor for how the reins and head serve primarily for direction, not propulsion.*

— This is a fundamental principle at every stage of dressage!

II. My horse will always move calmly and relaxed beneath me when I sit in its center of gravity, gain its trust, and do not cause it pain through the reins.

— Balance aid: independent of the hand! Trust!

III. In this balance, I find all the aids I need. I let my center of gravity shift forward, backward, right, or left—and then the center of gravity of the horse-rider system shifts accordingly, and the horse will adjust, turn, change its gait, or curve right or left.

— Weight aids are primary, because they are followed instinctively!

A horse ridden by a skilled rider with good conformation and equally calm and courageous temperament could, following these principles, perform almost everything. A few extended gallops would encourage it to lower its head and neck somewhat, whereby it would learn the comfort of a soft, elastic connection with the bit; its hind legs would then begin to step under more by themselves. Without knowing it, the horse would begin to respect the bit and easily shift into collected gaits through weight and rein aids.

If the rider now asks himself where the essential obstacle lies that prevents the average horse from being ridden like the one just described, it immediately becomes apparent: the significantly forward-shifted center of gravity of the latter horse, as well as the impossibility for the horse to bring its hind legs forward enough—due to its long frame—to support part of the overhanging load.

He will understand that, at higher speeds, balance is threatened from the front by the momentum of movement; and further, that nearly the entire weight falling onto the forelegs causes these to become over-strained.

So, the rider must now consider how he can shift this without violating the three conclusions already derived from the laws of balance, which are now recognized as correct.

He finds a suitable method in the ability to slightly incline his own upper body behind the horse's center of gravity. But he will make a peculiar discovery: the horse does not slow its pace, as would be expected from the laws of balance. Instead, it engages its hind legs more forcefully, lengthens its stride, and strengthens the gait.

Soon, this will seem self-evident to him. For he will notice that the hind legs are connected by joints into a series of levers and that the latter, with their numerous muscles, tendons, and ligaments, are equipped with a significant spring-like power. Every lever capable of elastic reaction snaps back with more energy the more tightly it is compressed—thus, by increased loading, the hind leg joints become slightly more compressed and consequently thrust back with more energy.

As a result, the entire body is propelled further forward. To maintain balance, the limbs must also reach farther forward or outward, and the rider—by issuing careful aids from within the state of balance—will, on the one hand, have slightly shifted the system's overall center of gravity, and on the other hand, have prompted the hind legs to push off more strongly and step further forward.

Now the rider will also want to shorten the stride again. This is where experience comes into play. It teaches that a horse,[5] when it is ridden in balance, without pain, and with trust, will loosen after a certain amount of time and surrender completely to its natural posture.

Firstly, this natural posture reveals itself as a long-stretched neck with a hanging nose;

Secondly, it shows that a horse with a bit in its mouth will naturally accept and lean lightly into this long-stretched position; Thirdly, it teaches that a horse will quite naturally shorten its stride again when it experiences even the slightest momentary resistance through the bit; Fourthly, that a horse holds it entirely natural to collect its movement when a light signal through the bit is given—without force.

A horse like this—be it a blood horse from the stud or a horse ridden daily by a country boy—demonstrates fifthly: that in the described state of relaxation, the horse becomes receptive even to the slightest, most subtle natural signals.

Thus, the rider will already have allowed the horse to softly lean into the bit with the long rein. If he now wishes to shorten the gait, he does so by lightly increasing the tension of the rein, giving the horse a momentary signal to slow down, without abruptly pulling—just applying a momentary suggestion.

If this produces the desired effect, the hand immediately relaxes again, and the horse returns to its light contact on the softly following rein.

Now, if the rider combines the forward-driving aid with a light suggestion from the hand, the horse's hindquarters will become more active and will step forward more energetically—but without increasing speed across the ground. The energy is redirected upward: the impulsion is caught and transformed into upward thrust.

At the same time, the contact becomes more influenced by the hindquarters. With some practice, the horse maintains this new, more powerful connection as its natural state; it becomes the horse's new normal. This forms the foundation for what is commonly referred to as "engagement of the hindquarters."

---

[5] *In this very general consideration, particular difficulties in conformation or temperament are, of course, not assumed. These will be addressed later. We are to think of a horse which, endowed with a calm temperament, after a few days willingly tolerates the rider and moves for long stretches on the forehand. Only with such a horse, which normally expresses the effects of weight, can the normal effects of weight be demonstrated.*

Although this process is frequently interrupted, it should always be resumed with only minimal interruption[6] so that collection and contact can continuously develop and become second nature to the horse. Throughout this slow process of engaging the hindquarters, balance on the legs and relaxation must remain undisturbed from beginning to end. At the same time, the energetic forward movement, as well as the elastic acceptance of the weight through the hindquarters, must steadily increase—to the extent that it is possible for the horse in question.

The back will become broader and more powerful, enveloping the rider more completely. The thighs will, as soon as the thrust from the hind legs reaches a certain strength, begin to work actively at the saddle's pivot point. The relaxed horse—because it does not contract itself and instead maintains its body in a natural arching form—broadens under the rider and steps through the swing of the hindquarters.

The thighs begin to yield—and now, together with the weight, they become capable of influencing the subtle placement of the hind legs, both forward and sideways.

The rein and head, however, remain as they were at the beginning of dressage: a softly following connection directed forward—a rein aid into the horse never occurred!

It would be a mistake to assume that the rein and head remained unchanged in the same state. For even though the rounding and forward movement of the horse appear unaffected by the softly carried neck, the opposite is very much the case.

The muscles of the forehand begin—initially by yielding and softening—to form themselves, and eventually take shape in self-carriage. The prerequisites from which the author proceeds may seem banal and familiar, but he identifies a connecting link that leads to new and comprehensive conclusions.

The muscles of the hindquarters extend into those of the back and neck. Strong ligaments pass from the poll along the entire spine into the hindquarters and end there in tendons. The traditional rider's division of the horse into forehand, middle, and hindquarters can easily cause one to forget this natural anatomical interconnection, and it may foster the illusion that one part can be worked on without affecting the others.

---

[6] *At first glance, the author makes the matter seem quite easy, since he appears to deliberately overlook the resistances in the horse which arise during this compression, particularly in the neck and poll. The following remarks, however, are devoted precisely to proving that with this gradual compression from behind the musculature of the forehand, by natural necessity, is first compelled to stretch forward and into the bit, and then to self-form upon it.*
The assumptions from which the author proceeds are extremely banal and well known, but he discovers a connecting link that leads to new and surprising conclusions. - The Editor.

And yet, not only does this anatomical reference show the unity and connection of the horse's body, but it is also confirmed through everyday experience with the horse—as it would be with any living organism.

A bucking horse responds with resistance in the poll and neck; a horse taking a powerful jump with extended reach stretches its neck and head far forward. A human being will, during motion, naturally incline the head and neck downward as part of overall spinal alignment.

And so, it is indispensable that a horse, if it wishes to bend the hindquarters, must also relax and participate with the poll. The poll must conform to this rounding of the spine.

Of course, in the earliest stages of dressage, the development of the "arch" may be too slight to affect the poll significantly. But here, another aid comes to our assistance!

If the rider inclines his own weight slightly behind the balance point—as we previously described—it has the effect of shifting the rider-horse system's center of gravity backward. At the same time, if he slightly slows the tempo then the hind legs begin to step more deeply underneath, and a new shift of the center of gravity occurs—this time forward.

The original, natural relationship between the loading of forehand and hindquarters is thus altered. And again, it is a self-evident law of nature that any naturally given position of balance will always be reestablished after disruption.

The miller's apprentice carrying a sack of flour will lean strongly forward; the brewery assistant pushing a barrel will lean backward. A maidservant carrying a water jug in her right hand will shift her body weight to the left;[7] the horse, climbing uphill—where the center of gravity is indirectly shifted backward—leans its weight forward. And likewise, its rider will instinctively lean forward, whether he is a highly trained classical rider or just a farm boy riding his father's horse to the watering hole.

What is to be emphasized here is the compelling necessity of this shift in center of gravity.

Whether miller, brewer, maidservant—or the horse itself—it is an unrelenting natural law; the horse, of course, only if the rider knows how to apply gentle aids and still knows how to prevent the forehand from rushing forward by using soft, regulating aids.

---

[7] *Here, the compelling necessity of this shift in balance could have been emphasized more strongly. Neither millers, brewers, nor servant girls—nor horses—are asked whether they are willing; rather, they obey an inexorable compulsion. The horse, however, only if the rider significantly reinforces the driving aids and yet knows how to prevent the forehand from advancing with playful aids. Horses under saddle are brought to quick and reliable yielding in this way alone. The author here has in mind only calmly developing dressage. He thus considers only mild driving aids, which may then evoke merely a "tendency" to yield. For comprehension, however, it is precisely the potentially compelling character of the effect of driving aids, in relation to the correct position of the forehand, that is indispensable. - The Editor.*

Ridden horses can only become quick and sustainably light in this way. The author here is thinking exclusively of calmly developing dressage. He envisions only soft, driving aids, which should serve solely as a signal for yielding, not as a forceful coercion.

For proper understanding, it is essential to recognize the involuntary nature of this effect. The horse reacts to such influences in a natural and instinctive way—but only when its body yields to them without resistance. Then, our horse will also seek to restore its center of gravity forward, to reestablish the familiar distribution of weight[8] between hindquarters and forehand.

Now, if the rider maintains his rearward-leaning posture, he will simultaneously keep the hind legs stepping further under. And if he lightly blocks with the rein against the forward motion prompted by this shift in the horse, he prevents the horse from reestablishing its forward center of gravity. The result is this: the horse begins to lower its neck and head.

In this downward effort, we notice, as experience teaches, that the horse begins to seek a soft contact, lightly leaning into the bit on its own. This inclination triggers a natural reflex in the lower part of the horse's head—particularly in the jaw—that stimulates salivation (beginning of chewing activity). All of this, of course, only occurs when the horse remains relaxed and submits to its natural inclinations—especially when the upper neck muscles are not tense and resisting.

Softness in the hand is the beginning and end of all dressage.

If we repeat this process—activating the hindquarters, stimulating chewing, encouraging the head and neck to lower, accepting the increased bit contact offered by the horse, and then immediately softening the rein, giving the poll muscles freedom to respond[9] —then flexion and contact will steadily increase, and this new posture will become natural for the horse.

If we ask ourselves what we have achieved so far, it is this: increased stepping-under and swinging of the hind legs, and thus a satisfied, natural reaching for the bit with ever steadier contact, all while preserving the initial looseness and balance over the legs. But what we have not yet achieved is the shifting of the center of gravity backwards, since we have always allowed the horse to equalize the increased burden on the hindquarters, caused by coming forward to the bit, through rein contact.

We could have achieved this by not permitting the lowering of the head and neck. But we did not want this, because we wished to avoid even the mere appearance of using the neck as a lever.[10] For what we now achieve is much easier, more comfortable for the horse, and therefore more secure and natural.

---

[8] *"Distribution of weight" refers to the natural balance between front and hind. - Editor's note.*
[9] *"Response"—the natural stimulus of salivation due to soft contact. - Editor's note.*
[10] *"Using the neck as a lever" refers to the incorrect practice of pulling the horse into a posture instead of letting it develop organically. - Editor's note.*

We have now brought the horse's musculature into a far more favorable state of connection.

As long as the horse, though moving with a long neck and lowered head, did so without true contact, the classical division into forehand, middle, and hindquarters was more or less justified. But a harmonious muscle connection throughout the body was lacking. That has now changed!

Through the increased stepping-under of the hind legs, the muscles of the hindquarters stretch and begin transmitting their tension forward into the lumbar and spinal musculature.

Likewise, the overlapping muscles, tendons, and ligaments—especially the long back ligament—are stimulated by the contact, so that eventually a gentle elastic tension results from the stretching. Thus, we have created an interlinked, elastic, and resilient chain throughout the horse's body!

If we now activate the hindquarters, we also activate the back muscles, which in turn span the entire spine and activate the neck muscles. Conversely, if the horse, responding to our always softly receiving hand, increases contact with the bit and begins to carry the neck more, then the muscles of the back and hindquarters also engage in harmonious, elastic contraction.

Forehand and hindquarters now support and influence each other, aid each other, and help one another. The rider's aids, applied to any one part, now penetrate and resonate through the entire horse. From now on, we no longer work just the hindquarters, and certainly not just the rein and head—we are working with the whole horse!

To quote Mr. D. Holleuer: we now have a "whole-body mover"—though still a long way from the final result, the foundation is laid. No more disconnected, mechanical steps under our seat!

Let us now return to our goal: shifting the horse's center of gravity backward.

If we drive the horse forward, we once again allow it to balance the increased load on the hindquarters by stretching more into the contact.

However, the tension now present throughout the horse's body exerts a double influence, significantly altering the horse's previous behavior.

First, the horse now becomes less willing to yield further at the poll, as doing so would only increase the tension. The horse instead tends to stretch forward and out of the contact, relieving the tension on its own. In doing so, it also lightens the rider's hand by itself.

This pressure on the hand,[11] as long as the musculature remains relaxed and supple, is nothing more than a naturally elastic tension within the entire horse's body—like a rubber band: firm, but elastic and permeable.

---

[11] *"The pressure on the hand" refers to the elastic feel of a properly connected horse—not resistance, but tone and readiness. - Editor's note.*

If the rider's hand now matches this pressure—neither yielding nor resisting too much—then the increased tension in the upper neck muscles transfers to the back muscles. These, in turn, begin to pull slightly, causing the horse's body to rotate gently around its center of gravity—the forehand lowers, the hindquarters rise.

"The horse is now on the bit"—in opposition to the hand!

If the rider now does not interrupt this tension through skillful counteraction, then on the one hand, the hindquarters can no longer ease the tension, and on the other hand, the horse will want to yield in front to release it.

It will be even more inclined to do this as the stronger pressure of the bit on the bars increases saliva flow, and this encourages the horse to chew more.

If the contact—which we affirm—was strong enough, the horse, as we have said, will no longer want to yield by dropping the poll further. That may now even be prevented by the rein hand positioned slightly higher, which offers passive resistance to the downward-pulling pressure from the horse.

In this case, the only option left to the horse is to retract the base of the neck, since the forward escape is blocked by the bit.

Thus, the horse has now accepted the bit, regained a soft and light connection, and has shifted the center of gravity to the hindquarters by lightening the forehand and bringing the base of the neck upward and back.

This final movement—retracting the base of the neck backward and upward—marks the beginning of what we call "elevation."

The overall tension present in the horse's body is now met by a counter-tension from the forehand, back, and base of the neck. This interplay, as already mentioned, forms the basis of all meaningful engagement.

When helping a horse that resists, this already became clear in the previous example.

At first, the arching of the back, caused by the stepping under of the hindquarters, spread tension over the loins and—since no yielding took place in front—intensified the pressure on the contact. Then the counter-tension moved back to the back muscles, drawing them upward and triggering the mentioned rotation around the rider's seat.

If this tension is now fixed by the rider's seat into back and hindquarters, these parts become more compact again and pull the neck muscles toward themselves as soon as the tension in front is released by thrusting off.[12]

The effect is very different depending on the degree of tension prevailing at the moment.

---

[12] *A very illustrative example of this reciprocal effect is given in footnote 85.*

Natural Horsemanship

If no tension exists yet (as at the very first riding off), then the arching of the back itself creates tension and flexion, affecting the contact. If the tension between hindquarters and forehand has already reached a certain height (the strongest that corresponds to the dressage stage while still comfortable for the horse), then each side works against the other, waiting for the other to yield. Finally, if one side yields, the other increases its tension, drawing the yielding one back toward itself.

Should the rider, for example, permit the horse's attempt to place the hindquarters high and the forehand low, without pressing with the seat, then—just as the back muscles now draw those of the neck along—the latter would pull the former downward: the horse would not push off from the back, but would instead fall onto the forehand.

Herein lies the great danger of riders who lack sufficient "seat." Work means "to drive." The result of driving is that, as soon as the hand, after achieving a slight yielding of the horse, is allowed to elastically oppose, there arises the mutual tension between hindquarters and forehand.

If the seat survives this dangerous moment intact, the rider has won. But if the seat is not yet sufficiently developed, and the hands instead become too firm, then the horse, which by nature always tends toward greater loading of the forehand, will transfer both the rider and his own weight onto the shoulders and do as it pleases with its freed hindquarters.[13]

Such riders may only be allowed by the instructor to ride the horse in tension for short moments, and he must recognize with sure eye when the horse is about to become high behind and low in front. At this moment, one must oppose the harmful back-arching with increased driving, a hand that elastically counteracts the mouth but deliberately yields slightly, and at the same time ride actively forward with firm leg and resisting seat. Rider and horse will then soon be corrected: the rider gains more and more seat by overcoming resistance, and the horse realizes the futility of its attempts to raise the hindquarters and eventually yields behind—and thus also in front.

It should be noted that the driving of the hindquarters, which initiates the whole cycle of tensions and counter-tensions, is always relatively slight, so that it neither disturbs the horse's balance of movement nor causes it any pain.

The willingness of the horse, its yielding to natural influences, is the first condition for effectiveness. As soon as a horse stiffens, holds its muscles tight,

---

[13] *One might here, without presenting a detailed anatomical explanation of the action of the back muscles, simply say: here lies in fact, with the enormous strength of these muscles, the decisive point for the entire framework. The muscle is equally capable of bringing the pelvis toward the breastbone as of the reverse. For the horse, everything depends on directing this action forward into the rider's hand: raising the chest. For the rider, the task is to prevent this (high, light hand), while by driving the hindquarters under the body, to convert the pelvis into the firm point for muscular action. Thus, this most powerful lever in the horse's body—the connection of the breastbone to the pelvis—raises the forehand, lightens the hand, and brings the horse into posture. - Editor's note.*

or braces against, these aids no longer function correctly or precisely, while in the opposite case the reaction to the lightest aids is astonishing.

One need not fear that the horses are not held enough! Once they are beyond the very first basics as back-movers, they can actually be held very firmly—not with rough aids, but with collection and assembling that guarantees obedience, agility, and quickness alike.

And in holding, it is not the strength of the aids that matters, but the strength of their effect!

With this we have defined the beginning of flexion, of elevation, of bending of the hindquarters.

To continue further we have no cause here, since all further schooling consists only in climbing, after one stage of increased collection has been reached, to the next one in the same manner, and so on into infinity, insofar as the impulsion and carrying power of the hindquarters permit.

Never forget that the secret of gymnastic work, as of all riding art, rests in mastery of the driving aids, above all the seat aids—not in the activity of the hands.

From the rider's standpoint there is, from the first day on, only one single goal: to drive the hindquarters of the horse forward and under the rider's own weight. This alone, as *causa movens*,[14] produces in the horse as secondary effects everything that people have become accustomed to naming through terms such as "contact" and "flexion." The horse reacts as a kind of defense against overloading the hindquarters at first with flexion. Then, when the high hand no longer allows an increase of flexion, it reacts with elevation, which at the same time initiates the beginning of bending of the hindquarters. When finally the degree of elevation possible to the horse according to length and form of its back is reached, then only are the effects on the horse exhausted. And only then do the driving aids begin to act at their direct point of attack: now they bend the hindquarters directly.

The old, seemingly paradoxical saying: "The path to the hindquarters leads through the seat; approach the hindquarters, and you are master of the whole horse!" suddenly receives a clear and vivid explanation.

The first part is thought from the standpoint of the horse, the second from the standpoint of the rider. The latter must, from the very first day, have only the second half in mind, but that also requires that the first is completed with understanding and correctness.

And thus we come to the behavior of the hand!

The horse, to put it briefly, requires time. If it is suddenly pressed into this work with aids that are too strong, not adapted to its sensitivity, then from the pressure of the unsuppled neck muscles arises pain, which results—e.g., with phlegmatic horses—in dead leaning on the hand, or with fiery horses in

---

[14] *"Causa movens" is scholastic Latin that translates to "moving cause" or "efficient cause" -Translator's note.*

withdrawal from contact, nervousness, and despair. This is why the saying: "The path to the hindquarters leads through the seat" does not mean direct seizing of the back with the hand! That would immediately bring about the same harmful effects as trying to form the forehand independently by the bit alone. The hand must never truly oppose when the muscles are not yet supple. On the contrary: as long as the horse does not voluntarily stretch, release, and form its back muscles, the hand must yield as much as possible—supported by the weight aids and measured driving aids (or, in spoiled horses, the spur). And even if it momentarily resists because the horse shoved too much forward instead of stepping under, then after success is achieved it must instantly yield again, leaving the back muscles to themselves.

The less the hand compresses the muscles while at the same time checking the forward pushing of the horse's weight, the better!

The former is ensured by the relatively high, light hand—because then the entire spine is driven under, not forced over. The latter ensures that the hand is light in total.

One thus arrives at the almost still more paradoxical saying: *"The higher the hand and the less it presses on the mouth, the sooner the horse flexes at the poll."*

But, as with every other principle, this applies only with a rider who drives. And driving never becomes as effortless and successful as when it meets a light, elastic, self-yielding horse, and an equally elastic, non-resisting hand.

Closing Word of the Editor

The author has traced the changes that occur in the horse's body—especially with regard to the shaping of the neck and poll—brought about by the rider's driving aids, step by step, and has, as it were, allowed them to unfold before the reader's eyes.

This inductive method was at first perhaps necessary in order to establish the necessary rapport with the reader, and instead of merely asserting, to explain and to prove. Perhaps, however, it is now advisable to repeat the line of thought also synthetically, omitting the reasons. It is infinitely brief:

All of dressage rests on two cornerstones: balance and correct muscular engagement.

In natural training methods (work from back to front), both factors always work in the same sense. The improvement of balance through activating and driving aids produces in the horse a striving for forward and upward movement, while at the same time creating elastic muscular tension between hindquarters and forehand.

If this is achieved, further engagement of the hindquarters no longer serves to improve balance through greater flexion of the hind limbs alone, but the muscles of the hindquarters, seeking muscular tension, draw the muscles of the forehand with them toward the "ground point," the fixed support for exerting force. The muscles of the forehand, leaning upon and supported by the hindquarters, relieve the forehand and thus release it, creating self-carried balance.

From this moment on, both effects complement each other so perfectly that they cannot be separated in their action. Every improvement in balance through loading of the hindquarters also entails relaxation of the forehand muscles. Each demanded engagement of these muscles toward the ground point as the "fixed support" enhances self-carriage and the improvement of balance.

At the same time, the horse's constant striving forward and upward ensures that the forehand increasingly develops an even distribution of weight, contact, lightness, giving, chewing, etc.—despite and precisely because of the fact that the horse only accepts the contact offered to it and not one that is forced upon it.

The terms "contact," "on the bit," indeed everything that relates to the forehand, therefore become superfluous. The horse, in response to the continuously driving aids of the rider, places itself in the forehand exactly in the way that the length, form, and build of the neck, head, and mouth of the individual horse correspond in connection with its overall conformation.

Chapter Two
The Back and Its Importance for the Horse's Gait

That the back of the horse plays a great role in the art of riding has surely been heard by everyone and perhaps read here and there. But only rarely has anyone in the riding arena heard it mentioned, let alone seen all instruction based upon it as the foundation of the entire work.

This silence about the activity of the back is very telling; it proves that true clarity about the function of the back has so far been lacking in the equestrian world. Indeed, most people have only understood this much: that a weak-backed horse is unable to carry a heavy rider, that an overly strong back easily ruins the legs and tends toward short, low steps, while a moderately soft back is often connected with much motion in the forehand.

Some experts may have penetrated deeper into the essence of the matter earlier, but generally speaking—neither in the authoritative textbooks nor at institutions where one might expect the best teachers—has the activity of the back and its overwhelming influence on the horse's gait and control been much felt or taught. Above all, there has been a lack of understanding that the condition of the back, its mere anatomical property of greater or lesser strength, is relatively unimportant; rather, the decisive factor lies in the activity of the back—in the functioning of the back muscles during movement.

The first to state this great truth positively and to deduce it from the construction of the horse was Major von Holleuffer, in his book On Pillar Work, and his theory of "oscillations" will remain for all time the starting point for any reform of our modern dressage methods.

It seems almost unbelievable that such a simple and natural condition for energetic movement as the activity of the back muscles could have remained hidden from so many theorists—still more so that, once expressed, this theory did not immediately break through with elemental force. Had not various schools of riding, and recently Riding Master Plinzner,[15] carried these same ideas further, the larger riding public might never have paid attention to this new doctrine, whose effects cannot yet be fully foreseen.

We too, to prevent any misunderstanding, owe our own views to the stimulus of Holleuffer's book. This chapter in particular contains almost exclusively Holleuffer's ideas, only presented in a different order and with a simpler reasoning. The frequent experience that intelligent riders who had read Holleuffer did not immediately become "back believers" made a more straightforward exposition seem necessary.

---

[15] *Editor's note about [Paul] Plinzner: This chapter was written before the appearance of Plinzner's theories; the mention refers only to the article printed on page 1 of the "Militär-Wochenblatt."* —The Editor.

The Back and its Importance

In short, Holleuffer's idea is that no correct riding, no truly complete and elastic forward movement of the horse, is conceivable without the uninterrupted, stride-for-stride and jump-for-jump alternation of raising and lowering of the spinal column and back muscles. If these oscillations are lacking—whether because the back is held rigid through muscular tension, or because it sags downward under the rider's weight and cannot arch upward—then the elastic connection between hindquarters and forehand is interrupted.

One part can no longer assist the other; the most energetic impulse of the hindquarters breaks at this faulty link, reaching the forehand weakened, dull, and non-transmitted. In short, each part moves for itself; the horse falls apart, and bones, tendons, and joints suffer.

The rider then feels every movement of the horse as either hard and jarring—because the back is stiff and unyielding—or, if the back is hollowed, as weak and without energy. His rein aids do not reach the hindquarters; his driving aids do not reach the bit; in both cases, the connection is broken. The horse can evade both front and back at will; true control is impossible.

The well-known division of the horse into forehand, middle, and hindquarters—which should serve only as a schematic aid to memory—becomes in practice a dreadful reality, while nature, which shapes harmoniously, knows no such schema but creates only wholes, unities, within which no part can act without the others.

Just as in every machine the most important part is that which transmits the power generated at one point to the place of its effect, so in the horse-machine the back—whose musculature connects hindquarters and forehand—transmits the activity of the one to the other and is therefore of primary importance. This is even more so because, on one hand, the rider places his weight most directly upon it, thereby hampering its activity the most, and because, on the other hand, the only natural and therefore most valuable riding aids, the seat aids, originate from it and transmit the rider's intent from his seat to the legs.

The importance of the back becomes most evident if we compare the horse to a bent spring—a steel bow or rod—whose two ends are represented by forehand and hindquarters, and whose tension and arch lie in the back. Every tension ceases the moment the arch is broken or cut through; the spring's force disappears. The stronger the tension of the arch was, the more violently the ends fly apart if suddenly released. Likewise, the horse's entire power, or rather the concentration of its power in energetic, elastic movement, depends on the spring tension stored in the arched back, which is released and transmitted to the legs as the back lowers again.

And just as all the forces of the horse unite in the spring of the back, so the secret of controlling those forces lies in how the rider, according to purpose, combines and regulates this spring's tension.

However, one who is enslaved by the many ambiguous, popularly misunderstood terms of equestrian language will never grasp this secret. We mean especially the concept of *"Losgelassenheit"*—suppleness.

Rightly understood, both the racehorse in full gallop and the school horse in the levade should be "supple," but the necessary correlate of this highest suppleness is the highest degree of muscular tension and activity. True suppleness means nothing other than the complete surrender of the forces to the momentary purpose, excluding every interruption of the continuous oscillation that waves through the whole horse from the hind legs to the bit. It demands not only that the horse cease all resistance with its musculature, but even more that no part, through stiffness, clumsiness, lack of elasticity, or lack of capacity for tension, hinder the free unfolding of its natural activity.

Thus, suppleness includes not merely the ability to relax but—at a heightened degree, for this is the more difficult—the full willingness and capacity for the highest possible muscular tension, carried out even playfully. Both must alternate constantly. Even the lightest exercise, such as the natural trot, involves the uninterrupted alternation between tension and relaxation of the muscles, which, like the pendulum of a clock, ensures the regularity of the gait.

Here, of course, the need for tension is small. But for higher performances—such as those demanded of the campaign horse in the collected or shortened canter—powerful impulsion, that is, powerful muscular tension, is required. If a horse cannot remain "supple" therein, it is only because calm, steady, gradually swelling, machine-like tension of its forces is not yet possible for it through lack of skill or training of the muscles in this kind of work. Therefore, if we wish to achieve "supple" collection even in the highest performances, we must, through systematic exercises in muscular tension, expand the limits of the horse's immediate capacity in this direction; that is, we must continually collect the horse precisely for the sake of suppleness.

Working with the correct concept of suppleness, we thus strive toward constant, gradual increase of collection; with the false one, toward mere flaccidity.[16]

---

[16] *Editor's note on the preceding explanations: "The foregoing statements, like those that follow, are especially correct insofar as they are aimed at instructors who misunderstand riding instruction—teachers who never really get beyond the natural trot tempo and always return to it as soon as a horse stiffens. In a somewhat livelier tone, he directed himself against those gentlemen who misunderstand Plinzner's system—those who harness before they have unharnessed and thereby make the horse stiff in the direction of its shoulders. If the horse is driven forward from the hindquarters into a light, high hand and under the rider's seat, both errors are avoided. One must first make the horse long, and then compress it again. It is this latter necessity that they fail to recognize. This is the principal mistake in the misunderstanding of the riding and horse material of the army. For to loosen a horse that has been initially "ridden toward the shoulders," in which the lower back muscles—serving as the "strongest point"—draw the back toward the breastbone instead of arching it upward, again away from the bit by means of driving aids, requires riders of exceptional skill such as Herr Plinzner himself, and horses naturally balanced, such as the riding school—but not the average remount—provides. Even the best rider will work comfortably and effortlessly only when the best-built horse is used with this method; otherwise, it does not succeed. Nowadays, the author, as I know him, would write in the same sense. For here the driving aids play the deciding role. - The Editor*

Of course, here too we must not rely on the intention of the textbooks, but on the results which theory produces in practice! And then we see that, for the sake of "looseness," the horses fall more and more apart from day to day, because seat and legs shy away from driving, and the hand is afraid to have to carry something. For if the rider were to do this, the two ends of the spring with which we compare the horse would be brought closer together, a tension would be produced in the horse, and thereby the false concept of "looseness," which imagines the horse without tension, with slack muscles, and a given-up back, would be refuted.

Thus the driving aids are again adjusted one against the other, and with the impulsion of the hindquarters, the counter-resistance against the hand ceases again. Then the horse is indeed "loose," i.e. without posture, and since practice, as is well known, makes perfect, the horse acquires great skill in falling apart, so that it even performs medium and strong trot, indeed even the same canter tempi, in this form—that is, with each leg working for itself.

That in these faster gaits the horse no longer loosens any joint, but, fearing the jarring, concussive impact and the danger of falling, goes with tensed muscles, tendons, and joints as a man upon ice, hardly needs to be mentioned. But it must be emphasized that the rider's aids for controlling such a horse—since they can never be transmitted from the part upon which they are applied to the others—must become extremely violent and, despite or because of this, can never precisely regulate gait, footfall form, or cadence.

How different it is with the horse that goes with the correct use of its back, with proper tension of its entire musculature! The whole muscular network is in an elastic connection that unites all parts with one another, and by virtue of this, every aid of the rider applied to one part is transmitted to all the others, whereby even the finest and most nuanced aids have their effect. This possibility of achieving effect with the lightest aids is essentially supported by the steady regularity with which a "back mover" works in the tempo once assigned to him. Upon him, the rider sits softly and quietly of himself. Mere tension maintains the gait, the law of action and reaction remains valid here as well, and just as the pendulum of a clock swings to the right and, as long as the weight of the clock remains in working order, necessarily swings to the left by the same measure, so too must a certain tension of the muscles produce a corresponding relaxation, which again evokes that, and so on, as long as the average tension imparted into the horse through the given composition does not change.

In the possibility of varying this gait-producing and gait-sustaining average tension of the spinal spring differently according to the desired gait lies, as said, the true secret of the mastery of the horse's forces.

If I, for example, increase the tension of the spring of the horse's hindquarters by sharper driving, this influence will immediately express itself in increased impulsion and corresponding strengthening of the gait, if I hold the hand so soft that, on the one hand, the horse can take increased contact as a natural counter-tension at the other end of the spring, and, on the other hand, is not prevented from balancing the increased load of the hindquarters, contrary to its previous equilibrium, by lowering the neck and head. The tension in the horse will at the same time increase, its expression of power will show itself in a more horizontal direction, in a longer stride, in stronger contact.

If, on the other hand, the rider tempers the behavior of the hand in such a way that he temporarily accepts the increased contact, but through steady resistance with the seat does not permit the shifting of weight from hindquarters to forehand, then the horse will push backward and enter a more collected tempo. Its expression of power will appear in an increased vertical direction, the horse will feel more collected for a moment, and then, at the hand, come up. Here too the tension will become greater, but with less ground coverage, finer contact as expression.

If the rider, on the other hand, first tenses the hand,[17] the contact will increase, the horse at the same time will press backward against it. Depending on whether the latter exactly sits down this counter-pressure or returns it beyond its own measure, precisely the first or last of the two cases described above will occur; whereby the hand, to achieve an intensification of gait, must not hinder the downward thrust of the horse, in order to achieve shortening, must resist until the increased tension behind, through the horse's backward thrust—elevation—comes to expression. If the rider finally tenses only the fist, without sitting down the counter-pressure through the seat, the horse will push itself off the hand, the hindquarters will rise a little, the tempo will shorten itself but not fall apart. The tension will become less, since the horse will engage the hind legs less underneath, thus arching the back less.

It deserves to be emphasized here that the horse, because by nature it moves with the forehand more heavily loaded than the rider is accustomed to demand, always strives to balance a displacement of the center of gravity backward by lowering of the neck and head, but not, conversely, to balance a displacement of the equilibrium forward by increased under-stepping of the legs. This it is not capable of.

A sudden displacement of the center of gravity forward (stumble) the back mover indeed equalizes with great skill by rapid bringing up of the hind feet, and so saves himself a thousand times from the fall where the "leg mover" would long since be lying on the ground. The back mover still comes just in time with the hindquarters, because his musculature is always "ready for action," and because, by the close connection of all parts, every misstep of the forehand

---

[17] *Here the author evidently speaks of horses trained as "back movers." In them the harmony between hindquarters and forehand, horse and rider, is indeed so completely present that it is indifferent whether one first increases tension in front or behind. The counteraction at the other end is almost instinctively performed by both parts. Woe, however, if one were to apply this to horses still at the beginning of dressage! The author himself lays a distinct warning against such misunderstanding in the sentence that follows, which he immediately applies from experience. - The Editor.*

The Back and its Importance

instinctively comes to the consciousness, as it were, of the hindquarters. The shoulder mover, however, does not have his musculature prepared for every unforeseen event. Before his hindquarters bring the more or less inactive back muscles into activity to maintain the falling forehand, he is already down!

Otherwise, the last case—tensing the hand without any sitting down through the seat—is not only familiar to the habitual military rider, but also, since one often comes in terrain into the situation of letting one's horse go intentionally in a lesser degree of collection for the sake of greater endurance. Naturally, even in the ordinary gait, the back mover is much surer on his legs than the shoulder mover; the correctly working back muscles enable the horse in every situation to transmit his will from the hindquarters—by their inclined position capable of yielding toward the ground—to the forehand.

Naturally, even in the ordinary course of movement, the back-moving horse is far more secure on his legs than the thigh-moving horse; the correctly working back muscles enable the horse, in every situation, to transmit his will from the powerful hindquarters—inclined forward toward the ground and thereby capable of lifting the forehand—to the forehand with the speed of thought.

Still more important, however, is the conservation of the horse, which proceeds from the back, in contrast to the leg-mover! What, then, suffers in the horse primarily through use? The tendons—and above all the joints! If the back-mover is strengthened through his schooling in the arena, which forces him to go continuously with elastically working muscles and tendons, then he enters the practical demands of terrain riding precisely in a reinforced condition; whereas the thigh-mover, who has merely flung his legs slackly and without energy in the arena, has at best his good natural disposition to thank—not his training—if he does not break down at the first more serious exertion.

And now the joints! Through what are they ruined so often and so prematurely—especially the fetlocks? Only through unmediated, jarring blows, or blows striking them as a result of overly steep setting-down in the wrong direction at the moment of landing! Does the thigh-mover possess any means of protection here? No; for the only means consists in this: that the muscles and tendons which move the pedal are elastically tensioned and, through this tension, protect the leg like a rubber stocking, allowing it to set down gradually and softly.

Given the infinite harmony and the interconnection of all the muscles of the horse's body extending into the outermost ramifications, these muscles can only be tensioned simultaneously and uniformly. If the outlying tendons and muscles of the limbs—which are the most endangered—are to tension themselves protectively, then above all the most powerful muscles of the entire body, the back muscles, to which those are attached and through which alone they can be harmoniously tensioned, must be maintained in constant tension.

The possibility asserted by Mr. von Holleuffer, which may sound somewhat boastful to those not yet believers in the back-mover, namely that under certain circumstances crooked forelegs and still more damaged hind fetlocks can be straightened again through intensified training of the back gait, is illustrated by the foregoing. Only because certain tendons and ligaments have become loosened has the defect arisen. If the rider now understands how to increase the tension of the back muscles in such a way that it extends even into those tendons and ligaments that have become slack, draws them along with it, and brings them back into tension, then the crookedness is eliminated as well—and even if only rarely visible to the eye looking at the riderless horse, it nevertheless exists for the security and elasticity of the gait and for the feeling of the rider.

In the foregoing we have attempted to make clear how the most essential aims of dressage:
1. development of strength,
2. mastery of the horse,
3. security of the gait, and
4. conservation of the legs

depend in the foremost instance upon the co-use of the back muscles.

We must not forget, however, in these explanations, that the word "back-mover" ultimately remains only a word, which can and will say nothing more than that always the entire horse, never a part of it, can be worked.

The expression "back-mover" nevertheless does more justice to this requirement than any previously customary term. For the arching of the back is inconceivable either at high poll carriage or without the stepping-under of the hind legs. The raising of neck and head, given the S-shaped form of the spinal column, causes the back to sink behind the withers, releases the tension of the nuchal ligament, and thereby prevents the swing[18] of the hindquarters from penetrating through to the forehand. And likewise it is clear that the

---

[18] *In horses with a short nuchal ligament, the tension of this ligament—and with it the passage of the swing through to the mouthpiece (standing on the rein, back gait)— also occurs without contact. Such horses possess a capable back and good gait; it is therefore advisable to refrain from contact with them. Contact never achieves the purpose of improving the value of the gait. Horses subjected to the attempt become fixed in the hand, whereas in their natural head carriage they go entirely soft, yielding, elastic, and self-carrying. Contact is therefore never an end in itself, but only a means to bring forehand and hindquarters into spring-like tension. If this succeeds with firm musculature without contact—tant mieux! [so much the better]*

Only where hard, jarring steps are uniformly present—where elasticity, the principal hallmark of the back gait, is lacking—must contact also be sought even in such horses. But it will only be achieved by truly supple riders.

Addition by the editor:
At this point, I would like to indicate that where too much swing or excessively rigid back formation in dressage confronts the rider as a disturbing factor, the conscious, measured yielding of the poll is precisely the aid by means of which one is able to prevent the horse's forward drive without burdening the hand and without any expenditure of force, or to bring about the release of rigid muscles in the most effortless manner.

The Back and its Importance

arching of the back and the stepping-under of the hindquarters stand in the closest interrelationship.

One need only imagine that a horse, while standing, places the hind feet step by step forward up to the forefeet, in order to understand that the back must necessarily and gradually assume the form of a completely arched line, whereas placing the hind legs backward lowers the back and bends it hollow.

It is also important in another respect that, through the designation "back-mover," attention is immediately directed to the back. For, as already stated, the rider's weight acts directly upon the back, thus weakening and paralyzing its natural function most readily, but on the other hand it conveys to the horse the aids of the seat, which are, after all, the most natural and therefore the most valuable and indispensable for dressage. Therefore, all individualization, insofar as the horse is concerned, lies in the correct recognition of the faults of its back activity; insofar as the rider is concerned, in the correct evaluation of the seat aids on the basis of and in accordance with the back conditions present in each individual case. And ultimately, the whole of horsemanship lies in individualization.

We therefore believe that Mr. von Hollenffer has also made a very skillful and fortunate choice formally with the designation "back mover."

Editor's Closing Word

As already indicated in a note in Chapter 2, the importance of the arching activity of the back muscles had to be emphasized much more sharply and discussed more thoroughly. For here we are dealing with the most powerful muscles of the horse's body, surpassing all others far in strength and resistance, namely the lower[19] back muscles.

These contract when the back arches; however, they must stretch and extend strongly if the back were to hollow. Now, however, according to the author's own words, the back mover requires the application of both activities for every performance, even the smallest. If the muscles are by nature too stiff, too tight in their texture, then it is impossible to arch successfully before the hollowing, which, as the author himself rightly says, is much easier to achieve, has been ensured.

If this is nevertheless attempted, then the oscillations break at the stiff connecting link in exactly the same way as they are not further conveyed by muscles that are too slack. If, on the other hand, resistance is offered, then the stiff muscles find in the hand the desired counter-support, against which they increasingly and more persistently brace themselves.

---

[19] *In order to cite just one example of their almost superhuman strength, I recall the well-known* fact that Thoroughbreds, during operations while lying down, frequently break their own backs, solely through the powerful tension of these muscles.

I shall return to the correct treatment of the overly stiff back in chapter three, since the author himself there only later expresses himself more fully on this point; but I would like to add that I have missed a highly important "natural" effect not only here, but already in chapter one for the questions discussed there, in what otherwise seems to me an unobjectionable line of argument. It stands, to be sure, in the background of the discussions, is also indicated, but is not emphasized with the emphasis it deserves.

I mean the proof that a shaping of the horse's muscles, sparing and effortless for both parties, can only take place after preceding loosening, as well as a reasoned statement of how this occurs in the most natural manner.

Admittedly, one can hardly speak of a proof for the former; for it is quite obvious that long-stretched muscles can easily be brought into any desired form, whereas muscles already compressed tightly into a particular form cannot. It is equally beyond doubt that muscles which move freely and extensively in some manner yield more willingly and playfully to another movement than muscles which, held rigid either within themselves or by the rider's hand, show little or no movement at all.

Regarding the "how," the author has himself expressed his views in another essay lying before me, and I gladly give him the floor here, since it becomes clear from it that he too regarded the complete loosening of the horse as a *conditio sine qua non* [a condition without which it could not be]. He says:

"Finally, and this is the strongest reason,[20] *through the initially greatest possible withdrawal of rein contact I provide a very effective aid to loosening, which, in connection with extended reprises, even assumes a swinging character.*

"Namely, by granting rein contact the horse finds a point outside its body against which it can continue to tension even its muscles that were at first still held fast, much like an outstretched arm already finds a supporting thread. But just as the completely freely held arm of even the strongest man becomes exhausted after a few minutes, so too will the horse not be able to sustain the tension for long. What can it actually tension? Only the back, since the neck floats freely; but if it finds no point outside its body to serve as counter-support for the muscles, it will not endure this for long either, especially when it is ridden forward in a swinging gait.

"This view is therefore also shared on all sides insofar as everyone admits that strong trot cannot be ridden without powerful rein tension. The horse therefore requires strong contact in order, at the firm point outside (bit or hand), to tension the muscles of the back and hindquarters more strongly in a springing and oscillating manner.

"The same logic that induces us here to tension the loosened muscles in a useful manner for our purpose should forbid us from offering the unloosened, improperly held muscles a desired, indeed indispensable, point of support for their capacity for tension."

---

[20] *For the superiority of work from back to front over that from front to back.*

I have only to add that, once equilibrium on the four legs has thus been found—this being the true meaning of the ability to maintain tempo despite the lightest rein influence—the strongest means for complete loosening and stretching is again to be found solely in the driving aids.

Chapter Three
The Rider's Aids and Their Relationship to the Horse's Movements

The statement with which the previous chapter concluded: *"And in individualization ultimately lies the whole of horsemanship"* already implicitly contains the further truth: *"There are no standard aids for all horses; rather, the rider must, in each individual case, know how to select from all the aids at his disposal those that are appropriate and effective."*

Unfortunately, until now one has contented oneself with tailoring the aids, as it were, for a normally going horse; the younger rider merely learns how he would have to influence this never-existing normal animal.

This procedure leads to schematism and riding devoid of feeling!

One easily forgets to examine whether the so-called normal aid is appropriate in the particular case at hand; indeed, there are even riders, or instructors, who see the salvation of horsemanship entirely in the outward application of the bodily posture, head setting, etc., prescribed by the normal aid. Here too, form takes the place of substance!

The deficiency is admittedly easier to recognize than to remedy! For the infinite diversity of rider and horse individualities gives rise to just as many different kinds of aids.

One must, honestly speaking, concede that only in the arena, on the individual horse, can the correct aids be taught. And yet theory, within its own domain—the general—can also intervene beneficially!

The essence of the aids, the manner in which their effect upon the horse comes about, the relationship of the aids to one another, the limits of the activity of each individual aid—all of this is by no means so firmly established that a genuine grounding of the aids, derived from the natural conditions of the horse that carries a rider, would already exist.

Such a grounding would, however, provide effective protection against the dangers inherent in the normal aids. For, as everywhere else, so also in horsemanship, the constant asking after the reason from which one acts excludes mechanical work that shears everything off at one level.

Even if it is not possible immediately to erect an all-around finished structure, we should at least attempt to gather together a few building stones for such a structure.

For this purpose we distinguish:
- I. Aids through the seat,
- II. Aids through the leg and spur, and
- III. Aids of the hand.

In the seat—when viewed in the proper light—everything lies! It acts upon the back of the horse and therefore orders or weakens the great connecting link between hindquarters and forehand; its effects are for the most part based upon incontrovertible natural laws, are therefore understandable and sympathetic even to the roughest horse; they can be given in the most imperceptible and most nuanced manner, and are finally applicable in every situation, so long as the rider does not vacate the saddle altogether.

They are conveyed to the horse through the rider's weight and are thus, in a certain sense, all weight aids, and are—if at all—mostly treated uniformly under this designation. We cannot, however, subscribe to this entanglement. For we see precisely in it the principal reason why such fundamentally different opinions prevail regarding the weight aids.

Rather, the character of the seat aids, the manner in which they come into being, demands that we again distinguish within them different individual effects.

For every seat effect includes several weight effects, which, however—and this is the important point—**do not all act in the same direction, but rather in part directly contradict one another.**

The same seat aid acts not only upon two different conformations, but also upon one and the same horse in two different stages of dressage often in exactly opposite ways, because the general conditions here bring one, there the other of the opposing individual effects more strongly to expression in the total effect.

Yes, even more! The same rider on the same horse in the same stage of dressage will have to bring entirely different seat effects into play—not merely quantitatively, but indeed of a qualitatively different nature—depending on whether we imagine him riding at 100 kg [220 lbs.] or at 50 kg [110 lbs.] body weight.

In order to have short, manageable expressions and to be able to dispense with lengthy descriptions, we wish to distinguish the total effect—thus that which one has previously been accustomed to designate simply as "weight effect"—within the seat aids into:
- I. the weight effect,
- II. the seat [pelvic] effect,
- III. the action of the [rider's] loins (*Kreuzwirkung*).

By weight effect we understand the effect which the rider is able to exert upon the alteration of the horse's center of gravity, and thereby upon its gait, through shifting his own center of gravity—quite regardless of whether he is, for example, standing completely in the stirrups or sitting down as heavily as possible.

By seat effect we understand the effect which, entirely apart from any center-of-gravity shift possibly associated with it, the presence of the rider's load—respectively his greater or lesser sitting-in—has upon the activity of the back and the hind legs.

By bracing effect, finally, we understand the effect which the rider must exert in order to maintain constantly the presently existing center-of-gravity position and the presently existing seat pressure.

We are fully conscious here that the boundaries of these three domains are extremely fluid.

We further freely concede that in practice all three effects, separated in theory, are always found united simultaneously in one seat aid.

But the rider can, corresponding to the momentary purpose, dose each seat aid differently from the three individual effects—as, for example, it is immediately clear to every rider that a jockey in a race must often ride with a far-forward center of gravity, with the conceivably greatest minimum of seat, but with the greatest expenditure of bracing effect; whereas highly collected gaits, by contrast, can only be ridden with a well-held-back center of gravity, an almost completely released bracing that springs into the movement of the horse, and—at least in certain moments—a strongly deep-sitting seat.

This multiplicity in the dosing of the seat aids first creates their enormous, never-failing versatility, and the so-called rider's feel is nothing other than the ability, heightened through manifold practice to infallibility, to dose this correctly for the individual case.

We therefore cannot dispense with this threefold division and also hope that the course of the exposition will show that it is not merely empty hair-splitting.

I. The Weight Effect.

The prerequisite for weight aids is the balanced seat. This requires that the rider adapt his center of gravity to that of the horse in such a way that both coincide, for practical purposes—that is, for the rider's feeling as well as for the horse's capacity for perception.

Only then will the horse carry the rider calmly and softly[21] and this in turn is the prerequisite for calm, decisively effective aids through shifts of the center of gravity. A horse that rushes forward and plunges into the bridle is not accessible to them in a dressage sense.

If the rider now, from this balanced seat, intentionally and purposefully brings his center of gravity into contradiction with that of the horse, then the center-of-gravity position of the entire rider–horse system is altered, and according to the known laws of equilibrium a compensation must take place.

This compensation can occur either by the horse shifting its own center of gravity by the same amount in the opposite direction and continuing to work

---

[21] *From this explanation of the balanced seat it follows that the seat effect, as well as all* other aids, must not disturb the horse. The balanced seat is therefore, conversely, also the prerequisite for all effects whatsoever.

forward unchanged with its supports (the legs), or by the horse accommodating itself to the new center of gravity with its supports—i.e., by changing its gait.

The first possibility plays a major role in dressage insofar as the rider is able to prevent the change of gait and thereby induce the horse to compensate in the opposite sense, as we saw in chapter one.

The entire weight work, as we attempted to describe it there, essentially consisted solely in working over that weight which we intentionally transfer, through driving aids that initially shift the center of gravity backward, from the hindquarters to the forehand.

The second possibility gives us driving, restraining, right-driving, and left-driving aids, depending on whether the rider allows his weight to step forward, backward, right, or left out of the balanced seat.

We believe that with regard to the three last-named aids no contradiction need be feared, but that the assertion that a forward shift of weight acts driving may sound strange to some.

It is also only tenable when the prerequisite—that no shift of the horse's center of gravity compensates the rider's aid—is strictly carried out. We do, however, see the effect in many moments as unequivocal.

A horse that rushes forward—physically speaking: a horse whose center of gravity is unexpectedly and significantly shifted forward—helps itself through an equally natural riding art.

Rapid drawing-up of the hind legs.

The raw remount goes far beyond the track of the forelegs in order to reach the far-forward-hanging center of gravity in a supporting manner. And under the rider it is no different!

To begin with, the so-called "going along with" of the rider when strengthening the gait, when jumping, etc., is nothing other than this weight aid forward, only, as it were, in a negative sense; here it does not want to induce the horse itself to do something, but merely to prevent the horse, without it, from being disturbed in its forward movement.

One can see the effect of this aid clearly in a horse that executes the levade quite calmly. The farther the rider sits toward the withers, the farther the horse must step forward with the hindquarters in order to reach the center of gravity. One can verify this with certainty in front of a mirror.

This aid is also entirely valuable for dressage. It merely requires, as already mentioned, other cooperating aids (leg and spur) in order to deny the horse the possibility of bringing about the compensation by holding back its own center of gravity.

We shall therefore return to it in detail after discussing these auxiliary aids.

II. The Seat Effect.

If we initially leave the back entirely out of consideration, then the rider's load, above all in motion, acts driving upon the hind legs. If these, released, yield to the rider's influences, they bend more under the load, whereby in a natural reaction an increased, more swinging thrusting-off is brought about. The effect will be all the stronger the more the weight is assigned to the hindquarters, and all the weaker the less this occurs.

We here encounter the first contradiction between the individual effects of which every seat aid is composed. According to the laws of equilibrium, every backward inclination of the rider's weight should have a restraining effect, every forward inclination a driving effect upon the horse; as a consequence of the effect upon the spring joints of the hind legs, however, we simultaneously have exactly the opposite effect—there driving, here less driving, thus relatively restraining.

From this alone arises the necessity of choosing seat and aids differently according to the individuality of the horse, and of freeing oneself from the convenient recipe of the normal aid, which strikes everything according to the same pattern.

Thus, for example, a horse whose center-of-gravity position in itself demands a normal, upright seat will feel burdened by this to the highest degree if nature has endowed it with soft, extremely flexible joints of the hindquarters. Only a slightly forward-inclined seat, one that spares the hind legs, will here bring about calm and evenness of movement; every aid through backward inclination of the rider's weight, which according to the "weight effect" discussed in section I would have to act in a restraining manner, will only cause this horse to rush ever more violently against the reins. The seat effect upon the hind legs would here come into such overwhelming predominance that the effect through shifting the center of gravity would not come into play at all.

An uphill-built horse with stiff joints that are little inclined to bend may, conversely, perhaps be most easily brought into posture through good sitting-back. Here it would first and foremost be a matter of compensating, through one's own weight, the excess weight which the uphill-built hindquarters place upon the forehand. The driving secondary effect upon the hind legs could, due to their inflexibility, remain unnoticed.

Far more severe contradictions, however, are found in the seat effect itself, when we examine its influence upon back and hindquarters simultaneously.

Let us first assume the back in the form that is permanently hollowed by nature.

Upon every back, the load of the rider acts depressingly, and all the more so when the back is already naturally hollowed or has a predisposition thereto. It therefore prevents or makes more difficult the rounding-up of the back, and thereby simultaneously, as we have emphasized repeatedly, the stepping-under of the hind legs. As we have just seen, however, sharper sitting-in stimulates the hind legs to increased swinging and thus also to greater stepping-under. If we now wished to apply this aid to our weak-backed horse, we would place two directly contradictory demands upon the horse within one and the same aid.

We would call upon the horse to step under with the hind legs, but at the same time prevent this through the downward-pressing effect upon the back. It is clear that in such a case this aid is altogether unusable for dressage. Rather, the greatest conceivable relief of the back is required. Distribution of the rider's load over stirrup, thigh, knee, in order to allow the entire saddle surface to participate in bearing, is here essential.

This case is, however, particularly interesting, for it occurs only too frequently in the life of the remount instructor, even with better back formations. One very often finds riders who, to the eye, have quite a good seat, but under whom all horses become stiff. Upon closer examination one finds that all these people ride with dead, rigidly braced lower legs in the stirrups, while at the same time sitting in with the seat with the utmost sharpness.

What is the horse supposed to do under such a rider? Its hind legs are driven forward with the greatest energy, but where they are supposed to go remains incomprehensible. For the seat stifles every attempt of the horse to round the back. It can only step against, never under, the rider's seat, and that is precisely the characteristic feature of the rushing horse.

Naturally, in order to control the pressure against the hand, the reins must be taken ever shorter; to the pains in back and hindquarters are added those in the jaw channels, and the horse becomes stiffer from day to day. Even more peculiar at first glance is that such a horse, when one finally loses patience and seats oneself behind the reins, immediately appears as completely behind the bit. One immediately feels the deep hollow behind the withers, and if one now therefore frees back and hindquarters from direct seat pressure, the horse goes entirely without swing and energy. Most often the spur must then, step by step, springing inward, perform its duty for a considerable time before one achieves swing from the hindquarters toward the mouthpiece.

Upon some reflection, however, this too appears natural. For the horse previously went forward only out of pain, not because the hindquarters stepped under with swing. On the contrary, this has been artificially trained out of it, and only after some time does it succeed in recollecting itself upon its natural ability.

Everything that applies here to the soft, hollowed back also finds analogous application to the overly stiff back, insofar as it concerns the seat effect,[22] the direct pressure of the sitting rider.

---

[22] *Guidance and cross-effect will, however, be set exactly opposite. There: very low hand and little 'croup' (little influence at the back), because the weak-backed, relieved horse does not in fact press against the croup. Here: very high guidance and, if necessary, strong cross-effect, in order to counter what stiff-backed horses like to do—namely, to evade by letting the hindquarters trail off. There: deep hand and little 'croup', because the weak-backed horse, relieved, does not press against the croup. There: immediate collection, in order to push the slack musculature together; here: forward, free gaits, in order to bring the tightly gathered horse into stretching. Also, the entire dressage method is fundamentally different.*

It is generally to be established that for both abnormal back forms the actual difficulty is more or less the same. The deception usually lies in the belief that rounding-up would be more difficult for the stiff back. Yet we see, on the contrary, that stiff-backed horses preferentially place the hind legs backward, whereby the back rather hollows than rounds. Nor would anyone, in reasonable fashion, begin the actual work with a tightly bound back before the horse has yielded through free gaits and extended repetitions with long reins. For the actual work, however, the true difficulties only begin for both back forms when collection begins, i.e., when the back is supposed to round up beyond the measure innate to it.

Two qualities are required for this:
1. A certain firmness and energy of the muscles, so that even with moderate assembly of the entire body a strong, powerful, swing-producing tension of the musculature can be generated;
2. But also a certain extensibility of the muscles, so that the detours which the muscles must take over the arc of the spine and the hip joints during good collection can be performed without compulsion.

If we consider the form of a normal back mover, it is immediately clear that without significant stretching of the musculature running along the upper contour of the horse, this form cannot be assumed. If the muscles are too tight, they cannot stretch far enough to produce long, soft strides reaching toward the center of gravity; these latter will instead be hard, short, and tense. Equally little does tight musculature permit the lowering of the neck; the length of the muscles simply does not suffice for both. The remedy can only consist in slow, gradually increased stretching of the overly tight muscles, ligaments, and tendons, in order to provide them with the necessary freedom of play over time.

We can, however, achieve this stretching only through driving the hindquarters under with the neck lowered. Thus here too the back must round up in proportion to its momentary form. Here too, therefore, sharp sitting-in of the seat, bending the back inward,[23] can only be disruptive to the purpose of the work.

That this is indeed the case, we see clearly in our stiff-backed horse when we wish to induce it to elevate the forehand. Actually, this should be very easy for it, since even with slight stepping-under of the hind legs the muscles of the back already tense sufficiently to draw the forehand toward itself. In fact, these horses, when we shift the seat well toward the withers while at the same time allowing the spur somewhat more feel, readily raise the forehand even under lightly kneading spur pressure.

If, on the other hand, one sits heavily, or places oneself—like many riders—in the belief of thereby making things easier for the horse, close to the rear cantle

---

[23] *Does not occur in the "actual work" of which the author is speaking here, in any form of rein. The author evidently has in mind, in these remarks, riders who—even where the rein, if used correctly, would yield—prevent this through harsh, hammering pulling-in, as was described in Chapter 3. For such cases, however, these remarks do indeed apply. - The Editor.*

of the saddle, then all loving effort is in vain. Rather, the horses immediately become extremely restless, lash with the tail, strike at the spur, and would rather stand themselves dead than softly place the hind legs under. Nor does any horse become so firm in the hand at the gallop as the stiff-backed one when the rider believes he can hold it through sharp sitting-in.

While, therefore, the normal horse unites both qualities—tensile strength and extensibility of the muscles—within itself, the weak-backed horse lacks the former, the stiff-backed horse the latter prerequisite for a free, forceful, and at the same time supple gait. For both, rounding-up becomes difficult; both therefore demand the greatest possible avoidance of every disturbance through the seat when dressage with them undertakes exercises of the musculature—there in the capacity for tension, here in the capacity for extension.

In sharp contrast to this seat effect upon back and hindquarters, recognized as entirely harmful in cases of abnormal formation of the former, stands the effect which the seat exerts upon these same parts when the back correctly rounds up and down, or begins to round.

At first the hind legs now step under the load, yield, since they thereby already of themselves accommodate to easier bending, increased bending willingly, and are, the more pressure the seat imposes upon them in gentle moderation, the more powerfully bent, the more persistently urged toward springy swinging.

And not, as before, in an opposing sense, but in the same, supportive sense does the seat act upon the back. We need only think of the comparison of the back mover with a compressed spring, whose curvature lies in the back, whose two ends are formed by forehand and hindquarters, in order to understand the effect.

Every pressure upon the curvature of a spring produces tension at both of its ends, which, as soon as they are released, snap violently in the direction in which the spring was tensioned.

This pressure, producing swing, energy, and tension of forces, is precisely what the seat exerts upon the back that is rounding itself stride by stride; and when one reads the assertion of the old masters: "In collection lies all swing; even the laziest and slackest horses must step in it with fire and energy," then this truth finds its justification above all in the springing seat effect upon the rounding back[24] and the spring joints of the stepping-under hindquarters.

---

[24] *One might object here: "Yes, when the rider sits in upon the back, he acts just as hindering in the moment of hollowing as he does promoting in the moment of rounding." This objection is initially contradicted by the exertion of every correctly trained rider—but also theoretically, in the rider who is not properly trained—is primarily felt in the hands. Something of this is indeed learned, but riding is not learned thereby; it is merely learned how to restrain the horse. But the moment of collection is lacking; it is learned merely to pull and restrain, whereas the seat is neglected. The horse, on the other hand, has just learned to yield; the rider learns, however, under the influence of bad and*

Natural Horsemanship

Once the horse has first arrived at this point of balance, then in fact all active aids are concentrated in the seat! The strongest as well as the shortest canter lies in the swing which the seat, with resistance from the loins and the hand (both passive aids), is able to collect completely and securely beneath itself. Whether that swing is allowed to flow out or this one is playfully produced depends solely on the position of the center of gravity which the rider finds good to assign to himself and to the horse in harmony.

He simply tensions the spring in a horizontal direction by allowing the neck to sink while entering into the strongly forward-inclining center of gravity of the horse; by this he allows the hindquarters to remain long on the ground before they swing off, and swiftly like an arrow, secure like a roe deer, his horse flies away.

Or he tensions the spring in a vertical direction, by backward-resisting opposition of the hand, producing continued impulse up to the highest collection of the forehand; by entering into the increasingly rearward-concentrating center of gravity of the horse, he lowers the hindquarters from jump to jump, and in the most cadenced, most compressed canter we see the same horse return, which only moments before vanished so quickly from our eye.

And just as this seat effect completely controls the firm back-mover, so it also educates the horse on the lower stages of back action in the most playful and secure manner. Corresponding to the horse's point of balance, the seat[25] assigns the spring of the back and the hindquarters ever more work through gradually

---

therefore always new impulses, to interfere. Riding thus becomes a labor of the hands, at the moment of collection a hindrance rather than a help.
But if the rider is already prepared in the sense of the riding system, particularly in the gallop of the school, then the rider's seat, in its formal schooling, is trained by the gait; the gait, which forces the rider evenly into the saddle, moderates the moment of collection. These fine, immediate and continuous oscillations bring about for the rider the so-called "swing" of the seat; and this swing effects a higher degree of collection of the horse with the reins than could ever be achieved by the reins alone.

[25] *Quite true, but still easily misunderstood! The pressure of the seat is minimal, because in this stage of the beginning back action, balance and muscle tension in their effect (raising of the forehand through the hindquarters) flow together into one (Chapter 1), and then the mere thought of an aid already brings about its effect. Moreover, the horse lifts the rider slightly upward through the good engagement of the hindquarters (the creation of the rider aid known as the "bridle step" by the horse), and only in proportion to this increased average seat does the seat press somewhat more strongly. There is no question of a "sharp sitting-in," as the inexperienced might easily believe. The author likely wishes to express the same thing in his remark on p. 57 with the words: "Our horse has, on the contrary, just learned, etc."*

It is also interesting that here the seat effect on the back and that on the hind legs flow into one another exactly as we recognized in the concluding words of the first chapter as necessary for the improvement of balance and the improvement of elastic muscle tension. The increased pressure of the seat on the spring of the back incites the hind legs to greater activity, and the now also increasing pressure on the stepping-under hind legs tensions the back spring again more strongly. One improves the other; the horse works itself.
- The Editor

increasing pressure, and thereby continuously expands both the duration and the degree of the carrying and swinging capacity of the arch itself as well as of its springing ends.

III. The Action of the Loins (*Kreuzwirkung*). [Rider's lumbar–sacral influence]

It can best be explained, according to the direction of its activity, by comparison with the Spanish rider, from which at the same time its independence from weight and seat action becomes clear.

For just as the Spanish rider, with his slight weight, is able to exercise neither a weight effect nor a form of seat effect and nevertheless possesses an intrinsic effect indispensable for collection, so too the action of the loins is one entirely independent of the other two seat effects. It consists solely in the tensing of the loins, back, and hip muscles whenever the horse, by boring into the hand or stretching out of the bridle, seeks to evade the rider's influence, and can therefore find application just as well in the forward-inclined seat as in the upright or backward-inclined one.

Just as the Spanish rider prevents every attempt of the horse to free itself from the momentarily desired collection, produced by correctly adjusted driving and restraining reins, when the whip aids compress the entire structure of the horse, so too must the loins absorb the driving aids and not allow the collection to dissolve. In this passive role the loins form an analogue and at the same time the correlate to the hand: they fix the tension and center-of-gravity position for back and hindquarters in the same way the hand does for the forehand. United, both hold the horse in collection.

As long as the horse willingly remains in it, they too remain steady and supple, also willingly accepting the pressure corresponding to tempo and degree of tension. If this pressure, as e.g. in racing canter, is very great, then the rider must also ride willingly with "much loins"; if the pressure is slight, then only "little loins" is required, until it finally lies in minimal tension, as it were merely on standby, ready to intervene if needed.

Every greater pressure—such as the normal one corresponding to the gait conditions—the loins and hand repel in the same measure, tensing themselves as the horse presses against them, but they also moderate their tension exactly in the same degree as the horse reduces its pressure.

Now the loins are by far the more important and decisive aid. As soon as collection becomes uncomfortable for the horse, it attempts, as explained in more detail in chapter one, a rotation around the rider's seat in the sense that it strives to place the forehand low and the hindquarters high. Only the loins, not the hand, are capable of effectively preventing this; for from the hindquarters, powerfully pushing off the ground, the pressure of the horse originates!

One therefore rightly says, when a horse correctly pushes off against the passive hand in response to driving aids: *"The horse has pushed off against the loins!"* For whatever pressure may still reach the hand consists only of the meager remnants of the thrust from the hindquarters, whose main force has long since been mastered by the loins.

The loins are nevertheless far superior to the Spanish rider, because they are not a dead instrument, but part of the living rider's body, and are able to modify their effect according to the given situation.

Through this ability they become the most important regulator of the gait!

At first, in the gait—especially in the canter and in the jump—according to the various moments of movement in which the horse finds itself, the position of the center of gravity within the horse changes continuously. The rider must continuously follow these oscillations of the center of gravity if he does not wish to disturb the forward movement perceptibly.

In addition, the horse machine does not always function without disturbance, especially in cross-country practice! Uneven ground, jolts, rider errors, fluctuations in the momentary yielding of the hindquarters, or advancing of the forehand give occasion to threaten the evenness of movement.

All such disturbances are absorbed by the loins through momentarily increased or decreased tension, rapid entry into the altered center-of-gravity position, and soft return into the old tension and loading relationship within itself, thereby securing the beautiful, uninterrupted, even pull of the movement, and thus resembling the valve of a machine, which harmlessly lets any excess of steam escape.

It accommodates all pendulum movements of the center of gravity in the force system rider–horse or counters them, and through all intermediate incidents maintains the actually intended center-of-gravity position and muscle tension corresponding to tempo and collection.

To this more or less active side of its effect, the loins naturally reach over into the domain of the other two seat effects. For this balancing activity is not sufficient with the mere change of tension of the rider's body alone, but also requires instinctive, momentary, and lightning-quickly alternating weight and seat aids.

These, however, are never intended to bring about a change of gait, but only negatively to counteract disturbances of the gait, and therefore find here their most appropriate mention. For the securing of the once-established gait relationships is precisely the characteristic property of the loins.

It is clear that each of the three aids can be increased from its finest, scarcely perceptible application up to its strongest effect; that furthermore each individual aid can be combined with any other; and that finally every degree of strength of the one can be united with every degree of strength of the other two.

If one considers this, one recognizes what an enormous variety of combinations of the three individual aids is possible in order to dose the total effect correctly in a given case. All of them stand at the disposal of the feeling rider, unconsciously and instinctively, as seat aids, to evaluate them according to conformation of the horse, temperament, stage of training, personal weight, etc.

Nevertheless, they are not sufficient—and this again proves the enormous importance of the back—for poor back conformations.

Every horse which has a natural disposition toward back action, a naturally swinging gait, could, in our view—if it were not a luxury—be trained and brought into collection by a good rider through seat aids alone. Not so poor back conformations! A deficient back formation, as we saw, paralyzes the most essential seat effect, namely the seat action upon the springs of the back and hind legs; it cannot be brought into effect at all or only to a limited extent.

From this point of view follows the justification and necessity of the aids given through the leg and spur.

These aids are, as is well known, developed from the whip aid, that is, through continual simultaneous application together with the instinctively driving whip aid they are artificially impressed upon the horse. This method is without doubt the most convenient and simplest, and there is nothing to object to in this. We cannot, however, reconcile ourselves with the view derived from this origin of the leg aids, namely that they are therefore truly artificial aids, merely conventional signals.

We rather consider their effect to be thoroughly natural. Horses with an innate back movement follow them—if not in the refined sense of the finished horse—nevertheless without difficulty from the moment they follow the seat aids.

For even these the raw horse does not follow without further preparation, but only after it has relaxed through familiar handling and long riding and places itself at the rider's disposal. And even then it does not respond to seat aids reliably or sensitively, but only when they are applied with forceful pressure. Even then, at the walk and still more at the halt, it follows them only when, with the help of the whip, it is brought into a stronger gait, where its balance is more sensitive and the gait itself already brings the joints of the hindquarters into spring, so that they become particularly receptive to stronger flexion through the action of the thighs.

Thus one could, with similar justification, explain the seat aids—whose natural and powerful effect we have recognized beyond doubt—as being derived from the whip aid. For without any driving means acting through the threat of pain—here the whip, later the spur—even these accomplish little against the will of the horse.

The customary development of the leg aids from the whip aid therefore does not in itself stamp them as an artificial product. We believe rather that the so-called campaign leg aids—although the high school does indeed partly employ agreed-upon signals with the lower leg—are to be regarded, so to speak, as a natural continuation of the seat aids downward.

Initially, on the straight line, the pelvis and upper body are set into motion by the movement of the horse, a motion which in a very shortened trot can be recognized as a rocking from one seat bone to the other. That at first the thigh participates in this motion through alternating increased flexion of the knee is clearly recognizable here, and even more so in a marching horse (we mean the walking exercise preparatory to the Spanish walk).

Still more clearly does the transmission of the movement of the pelvis to the legs appear in the loosely hanging lower leg, which swings pendulum-like against the rib cage and is pushed away again. In every carter who rides his cart horses home, one can observe this fact. One may, of course, say that the movement of the horse sets the rib cage in motion, which in turn sets the lower leg in motion. But the other view is surely the correct one, since even with a very tall rider on a very narrow horse—where the lower leg does not touch the horse at all—the pendulum movement of the pelvis and thigh still transfers itself to the lower leg, provided the latter truly hangs freely at the knee without any tension.

Likewise, on the curved line, or in the gallop, the withdrawal of the outer upper and lower leg is merely the natural consequence of the displacement of the seat which becomes necessary for riding curved lines or for the gallop movement if rider and horse weight are to remain in harmonious connection.

If we further consider a horse in shoulder-in, it presses against the outer seat bone, so that this gains increased contact with the horse. It is therefore entirely consistent that the lower leg—where everything appears intensified and more visible—also gains the firmer contact in relation to the inner leg which it ought to have in this movement according to theoretical requirements. At the same time, the inner seat bone, for the rider's feeling, will exert gentler pressure against the outward-yielding horse when the inner hind leg swings, stronger pressure when the inner hind leg bears weight; accordingly, the lower leg left loose to the horse's movement will, as a continuation of that pelvic movement, strike more strongly against the horse in the latter moment, and have looser contact in the former.

Similar explanations can be given for every movement, and thus we believe that the leg aid in its principal functions is nothing more than the downward continuation and, in its sense, the intensified aid of the seat.

This conception will—for a Darwinian at least—perhaps become more intelligible if we add that the true rider spreads himself in the seat so broadly that the seat bones do not merely have contact with the horse from above, but that each from right and left embraces the horse's spine and is thus actually capable of acting unilaterally.

This would then be, as it were, the origin of our oldest, still legless ancestors; gradually the legs developed, but however long they may become, the concentration point of all force and effect always remains above, in the pelvis and loins, which suffices equally for the longest and shortest legs, the broadest and narrowest horses—in short, for all conditions.

The purpose we connect with these explanations is to correctly define the relationship between leg and seat aids and to oppose prevailing false conceptions.

The Rider's Aids

The leg aids are, briefly stated, never primary aids, but are to be regarded merely as supporting aids. They must proceed from the correct seat, adapt themselves to it and subordinate themselves to it, and be given with the awareness that, by themselves, without proper use through the seat, they are downright worthless.

We do not wish thereby to diminish their importance. We even gladly concede that for finer dressage as well as for complete obedience they are indispensable with every horse. For, as already mentioned, only the pain threatened by the spur[26] guarantees full obedience and the surrender of the last possible effort. Whoever is of another opinion should simply ride once without spurs on a truly lazy remount horse. He will experience wonders, but at the same time also recognize how powerless even the seat aids are against the will of the horse; how indispensable it therefore is to have the good will of the horse on one's side—and then, however, also to break the will of every resistant horse.

This appreciation of the leg and its intensification, the spur, does not, however, remove the fact that successes through these aids can only be achieved with correctly chosen seat and correct seat aids, and that therefore only these remain the main aids, while the others remain auxiliary aids. It must not be admitted that in the concert of aids the rein and leg aids play first violin, while the seat resembles at most the large bass, which contributes least to the harmony of the whole. Yet if one enters a riding arena today, one hears much—very much—of hand and rein, some of the leg, nothing or vanishingly little of the seat and its aids.

This fact reveals a false conception of the essence of horsemanship. In truth, the hand—of which we shall still speak—has only a passive role; the leg supports the correctly placed weight; in the correct placement of the rider and in the seat aids given from the correct seat lies the true essence of riding.

The leg in particular should only help the still unfinished horse to understand effects ranging from mere contact at the hair to the most driving pressure and to transform them, again and again, into such bodily forms that the seat can take possession of them and convert them into something permanent remaining in the horse.

From this role of the leg follows also the generally recognized requirement that in the course of dressage the leg aids should gradually diminish.

One must always keep in mind that breaking-in is nothing more than a progressive fine tuning of the still incorrectly moving horse's balance into the gradually ever more correctly held rider's balance. Only then does one remain on natural ground.

---

[26] *Leg and spur are to be regarded as completely equivalent aids; the leg is the lightest spur, the spur the strongest leg aid. Naturally, the rider must be practiced in the use of the spur, and his action must be understood as ranging from the mere application of the leg on the hair to the driving pressure. The thrust with the spur as an aid is at most conceivable when jumping, namely over an obstacle that suddenly and unexpectedly appears.*

The effect of the leg when riding straight ahead is a very simple one.

It drives the hind feet under the body, thereby bringing about the lifting of the back when this is lacking, and now allows the seat—especially the effect we have described as seat-bone action—to come into play. Indirectly, however, through this driving under of the hindquarters it also brings the center of gravity back and thus acts representatively or supportively for the restraining effect of weight.

A quite special role, however, still falls to it in connection with that weight effect which claims to act drivingly through the forward displacement of the rider's center of gravity. We have already emphasized earlier that this aid attains practical effectiveness only where other aids prevent the horse from bringing its own center of gravity back by the same amount. If such aids are lacking, the horse simply behaves by stepping less under with the hind legs; it falls apart, especially since the seat-bone action on the springs of back and hindquarters is simultaneously weakened by the rider's forward inclination.

The matter appears quite different, however, when the driving spur is added to the weight aid. In that case the horse, if it is to reach the center of gravity that now lies farther forward and support it, must step correspondingly farther forward; but the farther forward it steps, the more the loins must arch, and the more we compel the horse into true back action.

Only for a rider with real feeling, who is clearly aware whether the horse—by means of increased impulsion (for this is necessary in order to allow the hind legs to reach the more forward-lying center of gravity)—actually goes forward or not, is this aid to be recommended. For such a rider, however, it is like no other second aid, precisely for helping the horse over the most difficult cliffs of dressage.

Both for the horse with overly soft, overly long, overly elastic muscles and for the one with very tight, overly short muscles, this aid becomes a true benefit and promotes dressage enormously. We have already shown, in our discussion of the effect of the seat, how indispensable it is, for both types of horses, to free the back by avoiding as much as possible any direct driving with the seat. Here the combination of leg and forward-shifted weight[27] aid now comes helpfully into play.

It allows the effect of the seat—which in both types of horses makes arching of the back and thus engagement of the hindquarters more difficult—to be neutralized as much as possible by shifting the center of gravity well forward through the weight aid, while at the same time, through leg and spur, the

---

[27] As long as stiff-backed horses—especially when they are at the same time built downhill—still resist by boring against the hand, by bracing the hindquarters, etc., a strongly backward-shifted weight effect may indeed be indicated at first. But once they begin to submit willingly to work, the same dressage method will also yield success for them. The decision in the individual case is ultimately a matter of feel: whether one must first compel the horse more strongly and set it into respect, or whether one should strengthen a willingly submitting horse in that willingness through the gentlest possible work.

The Rider's Aids

hindquarters are nevertheless urged to swing energetically forward up to that center of gravity.

The farther forward this center of gravity lies, the farther, as stated, the hind legs must step under; the more they do so, the more the back must arch, and the more securely we achieve true back action.

To complete the discussion of the aids, it remains to speak of the hand.

It is true that we cannot ride without it; for we need a point against which our driving aids can push the horse together. But it is only the barrier that restrains an excessive forward thrust of the horse—never, however, a lever with which to work into the horse.

As long as the natural desire to go forward of the horse, or the driving aids, provide sufficient impulsion, the hand has no right to exist. It has no right to press itself, on its own initiative, against the musculature of the horse. Only when impulsion reaches it from the hind legs—and even then only passively, through the simple acceptance of the weight pushed toward it—does it take part in the work.

In this realization lies perhaps the beginning of all riding wisdom. For the horse is not meant to learn, through dressage, to hold itself back, but rather to go forward resolutely and with impulsion. If we thus reject any backward working of the hand, we emphasize all the more strongly its steadiness at the correctly adjusted rein length.

The latter is correct only when the tightening of the hand at its maintained position suffices to meet any pressure of the horse against the bit—whether to increase tempo or to dissolve an already achieved tension between hindquarters and forehand—without difficulty. If this requires a backward movement of the hand, then the rein length is too long.[28]

For the hand could then, from the very moment the horse presses against it, no longer be "steady."

At this rein length, the hand lies soft and relaxed in the joint as long as the horse does not press into it. If this occurs, the hand must, in order to preserve steadiness, tense—or more precisely: if it remains steady, it will, without any deliberate action on its own part, be tensed by the horse itself exactly in proportion to the counter-pressure. If the pressure ceases as a result of the horse yielding, the hand likewise relaxes again of its own accord.

This steadiness in the latter sense—namely that the hand, when the horse relieves it through yielding, neither remains tense nor even retreats backward, but also remains "steady backward"—is almost even more important than

---

[28] Naturally, we are not speaking here of remounts newly backed, but only of horses that, in response to driving aids, swing energetically into the reins. Before this has been achieved, the hand can in any case only cause harm; it cannot therefore even be spoken of beforehand as an aid.

steadiness against forward pressure. Only thus does the horse understand that yielding at the poll and cessation of pressure are natural consequences.

That identical concepts apply to the bars of the mouth, and that upon this experience rests the horse's willingness in the most fundamental sense.

From the activity understood in this way, our conception of the "light" hand follows of itself. A hand which—unfortunately in the minds of many riders—is understood to mean that it should never have to carry anything, is conceivable only when a horse approaches the end of successful dressage. Otherwise, the horse itself determines the measure of the hand's resistance. If the horse is light, the hand is light as well. But what is pushed toward it by the swing of the hindquarters, it must also conscientiously accept!

Especially in dressage!

For a weak or only moderately strong back, the bit becomes, in a sense, a vaulting pole on which the musculature makes its climbing movements and through which it gradually strengthens itself.

The counter-pressure required for this must be granted by the hand, remaining steady in its place and willingly accepting the pressure. If it continually yields, there is no point against which the horse can tense its muscles.

But even in use, the hand cannot always be light.

In order to maintain the tension of the spring of the back, resistance at both ends is required: for the hindquarters partly the ground, partly the [rider's] resisting loins [and core].

The more of the hindquarters' impulsion is absorbed there, the more the horse tenses the forces of the back through the engagement of the hindquarters alone, and the less pressure reaches the hand. With horses that have a strong back and equally strong hindquarters, it is therefore often sufficient for the nose to be carried freely in order to generate the tension and thus the impulsion required for the desired tempo.

That is why such horses often press little into the hand even in very strong gaits, provided that the hand truly remains passive and does not provoke counter-pressure through its own tension.

Not so with the horse whose musculature has a softer texture!

For this one, even a wide engagement of the hindquarters is often not sufficient to generate the impulsion required for tempo; it needs rather a point outside its body against which it can tense its muscles, and that point the hand must provide. When the former type of horse reaches its highest performance, it too gladly accepts the aid that the rider's hand can grant it for increasing muscular tension: a finish with loose reins is inconceivable.

But—is it really the hand that has to perform the actual work in such a case? We say: No! It is also here the loins/lumbar-sacral! Because the hands are attached to it through the shoulders and arms. The entire difficulty, when a horse pulls, lies not in holding the hand still, but in holding the cross so immovably steady that the powerful thrust of the hindquarters against the forehand does not force it to yield. If it does yield, then the horse has won the game: for now it frees the hindquarters and pushes its entire, now forward-rolling mass irresistibly over the powerless hand.

If, however, the loins/lumbar-sacral area successfully dampens the attempts of the hindquarters to free themselves, then although the horse may momentarily press into the hand, it does so only to recognize its powerlessness against the immovable loin/lumbar-sacral area that absorbs the thrust of the hindquarters, and to push itself, with submission, away from the hand once more.

One truly need not teach any rider to tense arms and fists when the horse threatens to take control. Most do that only too readily of their own accord. The sore point in pulling lies for all in the cross—in the seat!

The hand therefore cannot exist without the cross. If the cross yields, the hand yields eo ipso. Without a good cross, a good hand is simply inconceivable.

Conversely, with a good cross and a regulated seat, a bad hand is conceivable only due to false ideas about its value as an aid—ideas that lead the rider to perform all manner of tricks at the horse's mouth.

In truth, the hand has simply nothing to do.

For the rein length is not regulated by the hand,[29] but by the rider's understanding—by his feel. If that is correct, the hand merely needs to hold this correctly; otherwise, it must itself be held correctly.

If someone nevertheless wishes to "round" the wrist in order to keep the hand soft, he cannot be helped.

The rounded wrist is, like many other things, a reminiscence from the period of the high school. It could be demanded there because a school horse never pulled, and thus never loaded the hand.

But it also had to be demanded then; for like everything that the old masters seemingly pedantically required, it had its practical significance for the horses of that time. The sole danger of the constant collecting in those days was that horses might come behind the bit. If it was possible to ride all the movements of the high school with the normal position of the hand, the proof was provided that the horse was indeed on the bit; for horses behind the bit cannot truly perform without slight forward-backward adjustments of the hand.

---

[29] *The author later, when he brought the utilization of the horse's lateral bend for dressage more and more into practical application, allowed the passivity of the hand to recede and replaced it, for his own person, with a hand that, swinging around its firm point of support, better stimulated and supported movement of the poll in the lateral direction. All the more strongly did he emphasize that any active backward action into the horse must always remain excluded; rather, one should merely redirect swinging back the pressure that the driving aids themselves allow to swing into the hand. Nor did he harbor any doubt that this type of hand action could under no circumstances be generally applied in cavalry riding, but at most could be permitted optionally to such riders whose complete mastery of the driving aids with merely suggestive hand action was beyond all doubt. - The Editor.*

Today, however, our horses often require a stronger contact, and with that the rounding of the wrist also disappears. A recruit who rounds his wrist certainly has no good hand. And older riders who ceremoniously carry their "light" hand before them like the Grail are always suspect. These worthy knights simply never drive their horses, from which alone impulsion of the hindquarters, coming up to the reins and then—against resistance—the working-through of the horse can arise.

They may therefore ride good horses, but they can never train, let alone create gaits, where nature has not provided them. This, however, is the sole criterion for judging personal riding ability, and this alone is dressage that truly deserves the name. Everything else is play-acting!

The rounding of the wrist is in fact downright harmful! For if someone places the hand naturally, as it was made, it is soft by virtue of the construction of the wrist joint and cannot possibly be made softer by any manipulation than nature made it. If, however, someone were to hold a puller for even a single minute with rounded fists, his tendons and muscles would become stiff—not despite but precisely because of this posture—so that little softness would remain.

We therefore believe that the hand should be assigned solely a passive role insofar as rein effects are concerned. Where such effects appear necessary, they will, with passivity of the hand and lightly continuing driving aids, automatically be referred to the cross, which redirects the resistance back to where it originated—to the hindquarters.

Nevertheless, we willingly grant the hand, so to speak, a shimmer of activity insofar as we like to imagine it, with all steadiness, yielding an atom.

Quite different, however, is the matter of the place where the hand stands. In this respect it must be completely unrestricted. Whoever, as a teacher, allows his riders only a single prescribed position of the hands often makes the work difficult to the point of impossibility.

Just as the hand is a barrier to the thrust of the horse, so it is also the point of direction for it and thus gives the direction for the assembling of the entire spinal column of the horse.

More cannot generally be said about the correct point for the hand than this: *"It should always stand in such a way that the impulsion from the hindquarters can spring into it as fully as possible."*

Only then will that which, at the rein, begins as work in the joints, and later—when neck and head yield sufficiently—transforms into work of the hindquarters, be brought to full value.

Depending on circumstances, therefore, the hands—or one of them—will have to stand higher or lower, close to the neck or farther away from it, and we must not curtail this right.

Only must the hand never shift from its side of the neck over to the other; for each rein must act in a straight line back to the corresponding hind foot.

Afterword by the Editor

The author's explanations concerning the treatment of the stiff back evidently suffer from a certain inner contradiction

This contradiction appears most sharply in the contrast between what his own annotations (in Chapter 3) assert in relation to the text itself.

In both cases he constructs for himself an "actual" [or "proper"] work. Whereas in reality, in his method, both flow into one another without transition, in that the "loosening work" develops entirely of itself into the "collecting work," he presents the actual work as being in opposition to the "introductory" work.

He presents it in the text in such a way as it would at least have to be practiced if one were to dispense with the loosening work; yet at the same time he emphasizes in the annotations the unconditional necessity of the loosening work.

Thus he himself is not entirely consistent, because although he suspects the important role which precisely the lower back muscles play in the body of the horse, and thus also for a natural dressage, he does not fully recognize it.

Truth is always brutally simple, yet it lies in depth, hidden from superficial view. With the horse this is also physically the case. One sees nothing of the lower back muscles and their activity, and yet their voluntary yielding in dressage is the decisive moment.

I cannot go into all details here; I shall make only two remarks: one concerning the build of the horse, one concerning the treatment of the stiff back.

The stiff horse and the soft horse are comparable in only one single respect: in both, the springy-elastic tightening and releasing of the back muscles, the back swing, is initially lacking.

But since the reasons for this are diametrically opposed, the two horses otherwise form the sharpest conceivable contrasts. Since we are comparing, let the contrast also be illustrated by a comparison.

The soft horse is the poor man who, simply because he possesses little, can also give little; the stiff horse is a miserly but wealthy man. Both therefore hold back their assets.

Whereas the former, even with the finest and best persuasion, can never give what is required, in the latter it is only a matter of making him supple. Then, he gives and can give beyond expectation.

As far as the correct treatment is concerned, the author quite correctly presents in the "introductory" work of his annotations the only appropriate procedure.

To remain with the image: one has the promise notarized, so to speak, to bring out the treasures stored in the back—that is, through calm forward riding of the horse on long, though steadying, reins that nevertheless allow every stretching of the entire spinal column, one ensures the yielding of the initially stiff back muscles with absolute certainty.

Only when this has been attested and sealed by the horse itself through the voluntary offering of full and broad acceptance of the rider does one allow the collecting work to develop; then one is just as certain of one's matter as with the horse that is lovable and ready from the outset to yield its powers.

I cannot, however, escape the impression that the author is not entirely clear about the emergence of seat influence even in this horse. At any rate, he has not expressed himself on this point. He considers much more only the effect of aids already present.

But even the horse with the best muscular tone does not place these at the rider's disposal immediately at the beginning of dressage; rather, it requires preparation and can be treated either incorrectly or correctly during this.

In some way—favorably or unfavorably—the back is influenced by the rider from the very first moment of mounting.

Therefore, the emergence of correct seat influence is at least just as important as the effect of aids already present.

Yes, one may say: it is the most important of all. For the most serious errors, and those most consequential in their effects, in the treatment of the back are made precisely during the period of the first riding. It is therefore worthwhile to examine more closely the development of the action of the seat.

So eminently active and influencing the horse's power is this aid to us, once we already possess it—as the author has rightly demonstrated—yet for its creation we can, strangely enough, do almost nothing! It can be created only by the horse itself!

With it the situation is exactly the same as with the contact! The more we attempt, as there with the hand, so here with the seat, to force it upon the horse, the less success we have! And conversely: the more we avoid accommodating the horse with the seat, the sooner the horse voluntarily grants us this most valuable of all aids!

In short, the horse must—just as with the hand—also with the seat, on its own part, challenge it, find it supporting and also embracing.

There is revealed here a very fine connection between the first two seat aids distinguished by the author, the action of weight and the action of the seat, in which the swing—the Alpha and Omega of the art of riding—plays the role of mediator.

The correct action of the seat thus arises entirely by itself out of the driving action of weight, as soon as the released and swingingly thrusting horse follows this aid, i.e. supports the forward-shifted center of gravity of the rider–horse system by further stepping under with the hind legs. The swinging, thrusting hindquarters thus step naturally into action under the seat, but does not fix itself; the rider's seat does not act in a swing-breaking manner upon the back and hindquarters.

The Rider's Aids

This insight is decisive for the choice of means to achieve a correct action of the seat. Just as we have learned to recognize a false contact, so there exists in the minds of many riders a false conception of the action of the seat, which hopes to improve the activity of the back through sharp sitting-down, wide leaning back, or throwing oneself heavily into the seat. In reality, however, all such aids produce only a hard, jarring back activity instead of the soft and elastic one at which the art of riding aims, and which alone can be sympathetic to the horse's capacity for feeling. They are therefore not usable at any stage and with any form of back elasticity to which the art of riding strives.[30]

On the contrary, one should strive both to place the seat as far forward in the saddle as possible, and from the very first day onward to restrict the thrust to the unavoidable minimum. We will then very quickly cause the horse to forget our seat—this is precisely what matters at first—not to disturb back and hindquarters in their natural swing, and to ensure the initial self-active establishment of the action of the seat by the horse itself.

If the horse thus steps under the rider's load out of its own impulse, then the rider has nothing further to do than to allow this to happen, through light playing into the voluntary lowering of the center of gravity of the hindquarters, then again to give with the forward swing, etc. There then arises—lasting all the longer the more—that intimate connection between doing and letting between rider and horse, in which it can no longer be recognized whether the rider, without active intervention, bends the spring joints of the hindquarters more, because the horse previously stepped further under its weight, or whether the horse diligently and willingly steps under the rider's weight because this previously bent the hindquarters more.

Thus, even in the horse prepared for immediate raising and arching, the active action of the seat forms precisely through sparing the back from premature direct loading attempts by the seat. In this the stiff-backed horse is entirely the same. It is therefore in fact incomprehensible why, for this horse, one should adopt a different procedure than for that one. Here as there, the horse itself determines when and to what extent the action of the seat shall come into effect; the stiff-backed horse will merely require somewhat more time for this.

Incidentally—and I would like to emphasize this—the manner in which the author wishes to treat the stiff-backed horse—driving the hindquarters with the leg, restraining hand, and inclined seat, a combination of aids which for the stiff-backed horse unfortunately often cannot be dispensed with—does not fit into his system, which demands the greatest possible self-development of

---

[30] *A very calm and soft further leaning back on long reins, best on the neck-released rein in rest pauses (walk), is for all horses, even for those with moderate backs, extremely beneficial. Often only in this way are the back muscles brought to full, comfortable stretching. The effect is the same as that of the strong gallop, which is known to have the same purpose. The horse's willingness in subsequent collection is here, as there, essentially improved. Even a disproportionately light rider can, with skillful and conscious application, otherwise make advantageous use of the above seat during certain periods.*

collection from the freely moving horse without tightening in front is otherwise always emphasized. If one accepts the former manner of riding for a moment as the correct one, his executions are even excellently appropriate. Their origin is also not difficult to recognize.

Anyone who has often and quickly had to correct spoiled horses frequently comes, for the sake of saving time, to take hold directly at neck and head. If a horse is by nature well balanced, thus merely working with incorrect muscular use, this path is in fact the shortest for the first-class rider, especially when he is completely master of utilizing crookedness in the horse.

The experiences gained with such horses have here evidently influenced the author.

I would, however, not wish to omit the indication that with truly difficult conformations the sparing seat discussed here has a great disadvantage: it enormously deceives as to what the horse actually can do by itself. Under continued rider influence such horses go through all sorts of things; left to themselves, the long-term results are often frighteningly small. For a military horse, however, only that has value which it can produce out of itself.

Moreover, direct work at collection costs strength, sweat, and nerves, which otherwise—according to the author's own view—cost almost nothing; for spur, horse's weight, and rider's weight cost no ration.

Chapter Four
On Collection, and the Rider's Aids for Achieving It.[31]

The theory of collection proceeds from von Krane.[32] Anyone who has read this profound thinker knows that, despite the luminous clarity of his exposition, it is extraordinarily difficult to understand. Even merely to grasp the difference between the position of the center of gravity within the horse's body (posture) and the position of the center of gravity in relation to the supporting surface (inclination into the gait) requires endlessly repeated reflection.

If one then studies more closely the concept of collection itself, which is supposed to be composed of the two concepts "posture" and "inclination into the gait," one usually finds that one has not grasped the two fundamental concepts sharply enough—especially when one imagines very specific horses and then wishes to determine, in their collection, what share belongs to posture and what share to inclination into the gait.

Nevertheless, up to a short time ago we considered the arguments of Mr. von Krane to be entirely beyond reproach.

The outstanding work of Mr. von Oettingen, *Über die Geschichte und die verschiedenen Formen der Reitkunst* [On the History and the Various Forms of the Art of Riding], shares this view and considers it necessary only to expand the concept of collection by introducing various types (racing, steeplechase, school collection).

The considerations presented on this occasion are extremely instructive and astonishingly sharply reasoned; they unquestionably belong among the best that has ever been written about horsemanship.

Yet we believe that in two points we cannot follow this work.

First, the correct point of departure has not been chosen in von Krane's explanations in order to justify the necessity of distinguishing "types" of collection. It is argued that von Krane's concept of collection is incomplete; that

---

[31] *The first part of this chapter is worthless for practitioners, since it merely contains a discussion of earlier theories. For those, however, who concern themselves with theory, it may be of particular interest.*

[32] Friedrich von Krane's *Die Dressur des Reitpferdes (Campagne- und Gebrauchs-Pferdes)* (1856) [The Dressage of the Riding Horse (Campaign/Field and Utility/Working Horse)] is an early systematic work on the training of cavalry and utility horses. Oriented toward military requirements, it emphasizes gymnastic schooling, responsiveness to refined rider aids, and the preparation of horses for service in formations, while taking into account individual conformation and natural strengths and weaknesses. The work anticipates several principles of modern dressage and is available today in digitized form through major German archives. - Translator's note.

his statement—"The agreement of the degree of collection with the strength of the required tempo establishes the balance of the gait"—is too narrow, and it is then demonstrated that the type of collection, as opposed to its degree, also plays an essential role here.

This is entirely justified; only it is forgotten that this von Krane statement cannot possibly be intended to supersede the general definition of collection cited shortly before:

"To collect a horse means to give it a positioning of the neck and spinal column as well as an inclination into the gait that corresponds to the demands made necessary by the tempo and the gait."

This definition, however, encompasses all types that Mr. von Oettingen now distinguishes so clearly and vividly. It therefore completely exhausts the essence of collection.

That there is something not entirely correct in von Krane's explanations is clear, but the inconsistency does not lie here; rather, it lies elsewhere. In a word: the explanations of Mr. von Krane concerning the "posture" of the horse, which form the basis of the definition of collection, are not only incomplete but also not entirely correct.

On page 130 of his major work, *"Untleitung zur Ausbildung der Kavallerieremonten"* [Instructions for the Training of Cavalry Remounts], he says:

"An 'narrower' posture would be one that brings the center of gravity toward the hindquarters; a wider, freer one would be that which inclines it toward the forehand; a middle posture, lying between the two, would allow the transition from one to the other to be easily effected."

Now, however, a very long-framed horse standing with extremely wide assembly of its parts—for example, with neck and head sharply flexed downward—can thereby shift the center of gravity far forward; at the same time, however, it can bring the hindquarters so far underneath itself that the center of gravity is again lowered backward by exactly the same amount. If both occurred to a high degree, then the posture, in riding terms, would be an extremely narrow one, and yet the center of gravity within the horse would not have shifted one iota toward the hindquarters.

If we imagine the center of gravity initially lying far forward, the position of neck and head such that the neck sinks almost to the height of the withers, but then the head alone is sharply flexed, we would have before us precisely the type of collection that Mr. von Oettingen presents to us as the collection of the flat racer.

Another horse, with the center of gravity lying in the middle, could stand very low with neck and head and thus possess, for a remount that has been under saddle for four weeks, a posture that is extremely favorable from the rider's standpoint and, given the circumstances, quite narrow.

If this horse were now to shift its center of gravity backward by leaving the position of the hindquarters unchanged but by strongly raising the neck up to

On Collection

the "stag's neck," then from the rider's standpoint it would assume the most unfavorable posture imaginable; according to von Krane's definition, however, it would find itself in a "narrower" posture because the center of gravity is more assigned to the hindquarters.

That this "narrower" posture, ceteris paribus, is also the one to be sought after in riding emerges throughout von Krane's explanations, just as this is in fact the case for correct definition of narrow posture in dressage.

Mr. von Krane simply did not think of such cases—indicated by us just now and capable of being multiplied at will through other suppositions—in which his definition comes into contradiction with the facts; as Mr. von Oettingen correctly recognized, he left out of account the various "types" in which a horse can assemble its trunk and collect itself, but already at the point where he sought to define the concept of posture.

The fundamental error of the definition is the assumption that a "narrow" posture implies a far-back center of gravity, while a wide one implies a far-forward center of gravity. In truth, a posture can be extremely "narrow" while the center of gravity at the same time lies very far forward (von Oettingen's racing collection); likewise, a posture can be very wide while the center of gravity by no means lies far forward (for example, a naturally well-balanced horse that goes long and flat).

From this it already follows that a correct definition of "posture" again unites the types of collection—which Mr. von Oettingen rightly establishes as a necessary supplement to von Krane's collection—into a single concept of collection.

If we consider, namely, that the back movement must remain present under all circumstances—that is, that the muscles running over the entire upper contour of the horse from the withers to the haunches must be stretched into a greater or lesser harmonious tension—then it is not evident how a flat racer can satisfy this condition and at the same time fulfill the second condition, namely that its center of gravity remains far inclined forward, without assuming an absolute[33] rounding of the back.

For since the entire spinal column, as we imagined our horse—with the center of gravity of racing collection corresponding—inclined far forward from the outset, then the neck lowered approximately to the level of the back, and finally only the head sharply flexed, forms almost a straight line, the muscles thus have only slight detours to make; therefore the stepping-under of the hind legs, in order nevertheless to establish tension, must be very extensive.

If the horse were now to bend the joints of the hind legs in such a way that relative rounding of the back resulted, then the entire hindquarters would sink

---

[33] *Herr von Oettingen shows in the course of presenting his "types" that for flat-race collection the absolute, and for school collection the relative, rounding of the back must be assumed in the horse.*

and the horse would very soon have to halt in its forward movement, because otherwise more weight would be transferred to the hindquarters than is compatible with racing collection. The center of gravity, whose correct position we presupposed, would recede backward.

At the same time, however, the horse must, because it still lacks the tension necessary for collection and for the back movement, step forward with the hind feet—and indeed considerably.

This dilemma can be resolved only if, simultaneously with the stepping forward of the hind hooves, every backward sinking of the center of gravity is excluded by a different positioning of the hindquarters. This, however, is conceivable only if, with every forward stepping of the hoof, the horse increasingly straightens the knee and hock joints and thereby gradually attains absolute rounding of the back.

Conversely, it is not apparent how a horse could arrive at the position designated by Mr. von Oettingen as school collection without passing over into relative rounding of the back. If the absolute were assumed, then the back, slanted forward and downward, would always shift the weight from the hindquarters to the forehand, especially since the highly elevated neck would cause the back to sink immediately behind the withers. The center-of-gravity position inclined more toward the hindquarters, which school collection requires, could not be achieved.

If, however, we imagine this as possible for a moment, then the hind legs would nevertheless have to step forward almost up to the forelegs in order to concentrate the center of gravity increasingly upon themselves.

Then, however, the muscles would be unable to lengthen to such an extent as to make the sinuous detours demanded of them by the highly elevated neck, the backward-inclining croup, and the hind legs brought forward almost to the forelegs.

Despite the impossibility for the horse of assuming such a position, we nevertheless present it in order to show how the two factors—muscular tension and position of the center of gravity—are decisive for the manner of the rounding of the back and thus for the "type" of collection which the horse must assume in every case. The conformation of the horse demands with imperious necessity that in one case the absolute, in the other the relative, condition occurs.

Another way of reconciling, for the momentary purpose, a far forward- or far backward-inclined center-of-gravity position with the back action is simple and unthinkable.

It is moreover clear that Mr. von Oettingen did not invent his "types" out of thin air, but likewise derived them as the natural consequence of the center-of-gravity position appropriate to the different purposes and from the horse's conformation.

Theoretically, one ultimately arrives at the same end result whether one accepts the incorrect definition of "posture" by v. Krane and corrects the matter again by introducing the three types, or whether one correctly defines "posture" and can then dispense with the types.

We nevertheless hold—and this is the second point on which we cannot follow Mr. von Oettingen—that it is both objectively unjustified to weaken the unity of the art of riding by setting up different riding forms, and formally dangerous to separate the three types of collection from one another in so positive and sharp a manner.

Without this separation, the riding world might indeed have been deprived of the extraordinarily high degree of clarity regarding the different conditions of back action which Mr. von Oettingen's work has provided. And the damage would undoubtedly have been greater; for we do not hesitate to repeat that, alongside Holleuffer, no work exists that elucidates the essence of the art of riding as clearly as that of Mr. von Oettingen.

Our reservations against the formally sharp separation also lie outside the person and views of its creator. Rather, we consider solely the effect of such a separation on the great mass, which readily reads such things but does not study them, absorbs them but does not digest them, and is merely glad to have found a new scheme, new catchwords.

The most striking illustration of the consequences is provided by the division of the horse's body into forehand, mid-section, and haunches. Have not even significant minds such as v. Krane, outstanding practitioners such as Seidler[34], fallen victim to the curse of this seemingly harmless tripartite division? Have they not, because of these paltry three words, disregarded the wisdom of nature, which creates only unity?[35]

Have they not introduced the separation of the schooling of the forehand, gaining of the back, schooling of the hindquarters, etc.? Have not these ideas of so-called systematic—in truth schematic—schooling of the noble animal dominated all riding arenas, military as well as private, for decades? And how old today is the clear insight, compressed into a stark and dry word, that from the very first day one can school only the whole horse, never merely a part?

How small is the number of those who have truly grasped this truth! And how infinitely vanishing is the number of riders who, even in their teaching activity, know how to hold fast to this insight as a guiding star and to transmit it to their pupils!

---

[34] Ernst Friedrich Seidler (1798 -1865) was a German riding instructor, Seidler owned a riding stable in Königsberg , where he became known for correcting spoiled and vicious horses. From there, he went to the Berlin Riding School as a civil stable master . He was a student of Maximilian von Weyrother at the Spanish Riding School in Vienna. -Wikipedia. – Xenophon Editor's note.

[35] *We speak here always only of the result of such books in practice, of their effect upon the great mass. From thousands of passages in the works of the cited, highly meritorious authors it emerges unequivocally that they themselves thought entirely correctly. But they have been misunderstood.*

It cannot be otherwise: misunderstandings are unavoidable, especially in the difficult field of riding theory, in which in a certain sense everything is right and everything is wrong, depending on the horse in question. One must therefore reckon with them. The inventor of such divisions is himself entirely clear about the inner connection; he knows all the thousand intermediate stages conditioned by the individuality of horses, and knows that the types and forms established as norms are only means to master the material logically, to structure it more clearly, and to bring it mentally closer to the reader.

And when Mr. von Oettingen writes:

"A school or riding horse must, in the highest collection, hold the neck and head so that the poll forms the highest point; the degree of collection must not disturb this relationship," we do not err in the slightest degree in our understanding of him—but we know just as precisely that such a statement, which owes its existence to the introduction of the three types, will become a stumbling block for thousands of riders. A horse might perform wonders in the higher campaign school; but if its poll did not form the highest point, or if another criterion of the frequently cited Oettingen table were missing, then perhaps precisely an enthusiastic follower of Mr. von Oettingen would say dismissively: "Well, that is all nothing; for a campaign horse in highest collection must ... etc."

There are, however, countless horses for whom the direct shifting back of the center of gravity through higher elevation is impossible, but who nevertheless fully achieve the required degree of collection through correspondingly greater bending and engagement of the hindquarters.

We hold the view that precisely the manner in which a horse wishes to collect should, on the whole, remain its own affair. A very short-necked horse will feel very comfortable if one leaves it this short neck as much as possible for the bridle and contents oneself with lesser elevation; in return, it perhaps steps far under with very flexible hocks and stifles and nevertheless places its weight to the degree required for highly collected gaits on the hindquarters. Another horse perhaps draws itself more closely together in its very favorably set neck and bends its stiff hock joints somewhat less.

In short, the horse, in its infinitely varied individuality, cannot be pressed into any schema of whatever kind; it hates it just as space hates the vacuum! And therefore the rider must hate it as well. Whoever enters into the individuality of his horse in this respect, leaves it to decide where and how it most readily wishes to collect, and merely ensures that, under driving aids combined with suitable restraining action of the hand, it willingly compresses itself through-and-through, will get the farthest.

Here is the point where what was said in chapter two about individualizing the rider's aids comes into play. One should merely observe under which combination of seat pressure, center-of-gravity position, cross-effect, and hand position the horse moves forward most decisively, collects itself most willingly; then the horse individualizes itself—and remains, what weighs infinitely heavily, always willing to work and ready to give everything.

But then we also consider it objectively unjustified that, by dividing collection into three sharply separated riding forms, one gives support to the still widespread opinion that a horse must necessarily be either a racehorse, a school horse, or a steeplechase horse.

Every horse will indeed have its principal aptitude in one direction; but why should a well-built, truly supple horse not today negotiate a difficult steeplechase and tomorrow show shortened gallop work in the arena? Why should the same horse not be able to collect itself appropriately both with a far-forward and with a far-rearward center of gravity?

That in the same horse the extreme opposites—flat racing and school jumps—can be reconciled from one day to the next is perhaps not to be asserted; but between them lie countless gradations which can quite well be mastered merely with a different "qualification." Just as a physically well-developed human being can execute a tremendous long jump over the vaulting horse and in the next moment perform a springy and elegant backward jump, why should the horse not be capable of a similar ability—albeit one resting solely on strength, bodily control, and correct balance under varying center-of-gravity positions?

The main point, however, is surely that the rider—who, as we said earlier, during training can ride today with strong contact, firm cross-reins, and a seat that promotes back swing, and tomorrow with the most delicate hand, supple hips, springy seat and legs—on his side offers the horse the necessary dual qualities to enable such varied performances. And such riders are rare!

Contrary to our wish, we have considered this purely theoretical examination of the concept of collection necessary, because collection is ultimately the foundation of all riding, and because without this introduction our still forthcoming own conception of "collection" might easily be regarded by readers familiar with v. Krane and v. Oettingen as superficial and written without knowledge of previous doctrines.

This danger is all the greater since here too we intend to cultivate purely practical theory, without stumbling over physical conceptual tangles—such as the position of the center of gravity in the horse, its position relative to the base of support, etc.—concepts which are neither made clear to remount riders nor offer them any practical benefit.

We therefore leave "posture" and "inclination into the gait" entirely aside and simply say: "Back action is collection."

The more the horse brings the muscles running over the upper contours of its body into harmonious, unified tension, the more strength these unite within themselves, the tighter the collection. The less these upper muscles tense themselves, the less swing and precision of movement they can develop, the lower the collection.

The muscles tense by stretching themselves, and they stretch themselves by the horse assembling its spinal column in such a way that the muscles are forced into large detours.

It is an entirely erroneous and practically destructive conception to believe that the collected horse goes "short" and the long-striding horse "long."

This is correct only if one considers the air-line between nose and seat bone; if, on the other hand, one were to measure the length of the horse following the crest line of the neck, the back, and the croup, one would soon become aware where the greater length, stretch, and thus muscular tension is to be found—whether in the collected or in the long-striding horse.

School horse, racehorse, hunting horse are in this regard entirely alike. In all three, in highest collection the upper muscles are strongly tensed, stretched as sharply as possible; in low collection they are relaxed and little stretched. And whatever degree of stretch and tension a given intermediate stage shows, that is how high or low the collection is within it.

Stretching can therefore only be achieved through wide stepping-under of the hind legs and a sharp taking-up of the reins from the front. There, as Seidler[34] has already said, the hip, knee, and hock joints form just as many pulleys over which the muscles and tendons of the hindquarters are guided over long paths in order to become tensioned; here, the attachment of the lower jaw at the neck provides the pivot point around which the muscles of the neck are guided in large arcs, so that they too are put under tension.

The middle portion of the spinal column simultaneously arches through bitting and stepping under of the hindquarters into that form most favorable for carrying the rider's load, and through this also automatically tensions the muscles running over it, which were already brought into tension as intermediary links of the neck and hindquarter musculature through their tension.

Whether the neck in this process lengthens more forward, as with the racehorse, or more upward, as with the school horse, or fairly evenly in both directions, as with the steeplechaser, is completely irrelevant to both the concept and the degree of collection.

Likewise, the position of the center of gravity has no influence at all on these two points. It only plays a role when it becomes a matter of utilizing the spring force concentrated in collection for a specific purpose.

For every specific purpose, every horse has only one correct collection.

But not in the sense that the individual horse has only one collection for all performances demanded of it; rather, on the contrary, the individual horse should—and must—be capable of different kinds of collection depending on the momentarily required performance.

With the proviso, however, that the horse adjusts its center of gravity according to purpose and its own individual nature, this adjustment is indeed of decisive effect. Only the theory must stop here and must not attempt to penetrate more deeply than it is able.

Thus it is worthless in practice to subtly distinguish between the center of gravity within the horse and the center of gravity relative to the support base. For neither the one nor the other can be practically measured or even sensed within their limits. Nor does it matter to rider or horse, once they have "shot the lark," to determine whether the center of gravity lay too far forward within the horse or relative to the support base.

Rider and horse do, however, clearly feel whether they are moving forward with too much weight borne in front or behind for the momentary purpose, and this center-of-gravity position, which presents itself as the result of the two individual concepts, is the only decisive one—even if it must be described in purely theoretical terms as a thoroughly unclear, blurred concept.

We can also come to terms with it theoretically without too much difficulty.

"A mass that is to be pushed forward must be located in front of the point from which the moving force emanates!"

"A mass that is to be thrown upward must be located above that point!"

It suffices to mention these two simple physical laws in order to understand that, for fast running, the horse must place its weight far forward, while for very short strides it must hold it far back if it is to make purposeful use of its collection. Otherwise, part of the muscular force would have to be expended to overcome the resistance that, for example, a weight held too far back would bring with it for forward movement, so that the force remaining available for the actual performance would decrease in strength or duration.

We need not, however, make theoretical worries that a horse would ever engage in such waste of force of its own accord, provided it is at all capable of collection—that is, worked throughly in loins, back, and poll.

If, of course, the necessary suppleness is not present—because, for example, the poll is not yielding enough or the hips are not supple enough to take on increased load—then the correct adaptation of the horse with its center of gravity to the purpose will not occur, but only because its muscles, tendons, and joints were not at all prepared for the suddenly demanded purpose.

A racehorse, even if it were very supple as such, cannot go a shortened gallop the day after being taken out of training. And one cannot want to send a horse that has only gone high school movements to the start tomorrow, entirely aside from its lack of fitness.

But if a sharply one-sided training has artificially unlearned in these horses the agility to adapt their collection to every change of tempo, that proves nothing! A horse, on the other hand, that is diligently worked in alternating tempos will, within the limits of its suppleness, know with great certainty how to find the center-of-gravity position that best suits both the purpose and its own nature.

For the campaign horse, this ability is of outstanding importance and deserves special attention in dressage.

We do indeed achieve bitting with a high, light hand solely through driving the hindquarters. At the same time, we achieve the elevation of the neck exclusively through the same aids, always carrying the horse somewhat higher than it prefers, thus raising it relatively—that is, in relation to the horse's downward tendency—always, even if moderately.

Once, however, we have made the horse secure in the loading of the hindquarters, so that we no longer need to fear the rotation around the rider's seat mentioned in chapter one (forehand down, hindquarters striving upward), it is time to alternate among the most varied degrees of elevation—from the highest to the lower, even very low ones—that is, with the type of collection.

By this we do not merely mean that we allow the horse, depending on the strength of the tempo, more or less elevation and a tighter or wider joining of the vertebral column. That is self-evident according to our view, and we have already mentioned it when discussing the movement of the back.

No—we now even deliberately create load relationships between hindquarters and forehand that do not correspond to natural collection. In short, we ride free gaits without allowing the horse to place itself as low or stretch itself as much as it would naturally do when uninfluenced, and we ride shortened gaits with a far lower neck and head position than is favorable and natural for these gaits.

How the mass of the horse must "naturally" lie relative to the point of attack of the moving force we have explained earlier in this chapter. There we already mentioned that only through the application of increased muscular performance can the resistance overcome that a weight held too far back brings with it for forward movement. It suffices here to recall this and the fundamental law for all relations between rider and horse: *"The horse is by nature more loaded in front than behind,"* in order to make clear the beneficial nature of a work performance demanded of the horse in this sense.

In the opposite case—shortened gaits with the horse in a low position in front—the benefit of this work is not so immediately apparent. Nor is a dressage advantage achieved without further conditions, but only if, precisely to the extent to which the forehand is permitted to descend, the hindquarters are stepped under and held down by the rider. Then, however, we also improve our horse in depth.

It must not be forgotten that the farther forward the center of gravity lies, the lower the neck and head are positioned, and the farther the hind feet must step under in order to maintain exactly tempo and the momentary load relationship between hindquarters and forehand. The higher a horse is elevated, by contrast, the less it needs—indeed, it can only—step under with the hind feet.

On Collection

Precisely through this work with a low neck, undertaken without diminishing collection, the rider forces the horse into the widest stepping under of the hind legs, bends them, strengthens and steels them most powerfully by increasing the load they must bear.

This increased bending of the hind legs will also transfer to shortened gaits at a naturally higher neck position; it will now become much easier for the horse to bring the hard-won suppleness to bear in the vertical direction as well.

Especially for the dressage of horses with short necks, great poll difficulties, and even more so for weak-backed horses, working in the strongest attainable collection with a low neck and a raised nose is of high value.

Such horses can contribute little to elevation, because otherwise, given the shortness of the neck, there is not enough neck remaining for bitting. While preserving the movement of the back, they can therefore concentrate the center of gravity strongly backward only through wide stepping under of the hind feet, as the rider intends—and they in fact demonstrate from the outset the impossibility of being satisfied with little elevation and relying solely on bending of the hind legs. Such horses themselves show us the true path to mastering their poll, along which one simultaneously achieves the greatest conceivable stretching and lengthening of the naturally short neck. With them, bitting is indeed produced through driving under the high, light hand, but then the descent into depth sought by the horse is permitted from the outset insofar as it is compatible with holding the hindquarters.

Moreover, this form is the one in which the horse "makes" itself most in the back. For the back arches most strongly behind the withers with a low neck, whereas every higher position lowers the back at this point more or less. Given the difficulty that precisely weakly load-bearing back forms tend to present to the inexperienced rider, this circumstance carries particular weight.

Once one has repeatedly and thoroughly had this experience regarding difficult necks and then transfers it to horses with better-set necks, one sees with pleasant astonishment that the entire fuss about poll difficulties is in most cases an illusion.

The deception arises because the horse in question is so little in balance on all four legs that it hangs on the reins. Its neck is then, of course, no mere appendage, as we demanded in chapter one, but the last support of the animal that is morally toppling forward at every step. Such a horse is always stiff, even if it were born with the most perfectly worked neck. There are infinitely more horses of this type than one is usually inclined to believe—and infinitely more riders who have no idea what driving with the seat and holding with the core (as opposed to the hand) means, and who therefore always sit on such horses.

One must constantly preach to them anew:

"In the deep stepping under of the hindquarters and in the complete yielding of the neck position—that is, in the driving aids with a completely passive, initially even yielding hand—lies everything."

Whoever has experienced this once knows forever that a horse strives all the less out of the bitting the more we lower it behind in the back movement, provided we do not interfere with the mouth and do not want to pull the nose in.

For the horse's striving toward its innate, natural load relationship—more inclined toward the forehand—which we explained in detail in chapter one, will always assert itself; and the more the hindquarters are held down by the seat, the more the neck and head will strive downward, thereby securing the bitting. We repeat, with full intention, for the third time:

"One thing must be avoided: attempts by the hand itself to act backward."

If the back and neck musculature are truly released, the nose falls of its own accord. If it does not fall of its own accord, then either the muscles are not sufficiently released, or the increased loading of the hindquarters has not succeeded for the still unfinished rider due to lack of driving aids or lack of 'core.'

There is no better receipt for the teacher that his riders are acting correctly than the falling nose. Since every further advance in dressage is brought about by exactly the same aids, one should never forgo this receipt. One then knows at least who is acting approximately correctly; whoever is not can improve the aids and thus their effect.

Even for work with very deep neck and head position, which is what is under discussion here, the latter must be achieved without backward action of the hand.

Here too the teacher must always pay renewed attention that the wide stepping under of the hindquarters is actually brought about through the driving rider's aids—something we ourselves will, even with nobler horses, rarely manage without the spur. For we do not assert, for example:

"Because the neck and head position has become lower, the horse steps further under!"

but instead we should say:

"Because the horse steps further under the rider's load, it places the neck lower!"

Which of these collections—with deliberately stronger loading of either hindquarters or forehand relative to the strength of the tempo—we combine with the natural one offered by the horse itself depends on swing and carrying power of back and hindquarters, form and length of neck, temperament—in short, on the individuality of the horse. It is the chief means of giving the horse confidence and ability to remain securely in balance even with a higher or lower center of gravity.

Only then do we achieve the versatility of collection that a truly ridden-through horse requires for the strongest as well as the shortest gaits.

On Collection

Concluding Word of the Editor

Of the author's explanations, those concerning the horse intentionally burdened too deeply on the forehand are, first of all, the most interesting. They cast characteristic sidelights on what is correct and incorrect in [Paul] Plinzner's system. The final result sought by the latter is also warmly recommended here, but firstly only as a dressage exercise, or for special (initially weak) horses; and secondly, the path toward it is directly the opposite. Here, collection in depth appears as the final test of loading for a hindquarters that has already previously been well engaged; there, the same appears as the first dressage objective, directed toward the shoulders. What this latter principle means for the average rider is particularly interesting. What occurs unconsciously with the average rider is expressed all the more forcefully in the sentence:

"Such a horse is always stiff, even if it were born with the most perfectly worked neck."

Even with a light, elevated hand—which prevents the horse from leaning against the bridle and leaves the rider control over his aids—the average rider often succeeds only with difficulty in developing that sum of driving aids which is indispensable for every method, whatever it may be called. But if, with immediate resistance of the hand, the forward-downward thrust of the still unresolved musculature of the horse is added, the horse lays claim to the rider's entire body, nullifies his effect, and pulls him inexorably onto the shoulders.

Quod licet Jovi, non licet bovi! ["What is permitted to Jupiter is not permitted to the ox." Meaning: the powerful are allowed what the ordinary are not.] *What benefits the first-class rider spells ruin for the average rider.*

The purely theoretical, often very subtle introductory considerations appear to me, in general, unobjectionable. Only at one point do I harbor quiet doubts—namely with regard to the collection of the flat (race) horse.

At first glance it sounds infinitely natural that such a horse must have its center of gravity low, so much so that it seems bold to raise objections. And yet I should like to raise them.

In earlier years I frequently had the opportunity to visit the great racecourses and thus ample occasion to observe posture, movement, gait, etc., of racehorses. I consider nothing more instructive—especially for the dressage rider—and nothing guards him more against one-sidedness than attentive observation of what takes place on the racetrack.

Thus I also frequently saw horses—particularly horses of class—in which the visual impression was by no means that they went deeply in front; rather, they appeared in canter as well as gallop to carry themselves completely. (Ilema, Privy Councillor, Omnium II.) That many equally first-class horses also pull strongly—I need only recall contemporaries like Nickel and Dalberg—does not contradict this. Horses with tremendous impulsion will always tend toward pulling; and since jockeys are human beings who act backward, one never knows whether lack of balance or muscular resistance against the hand causes the pulling. Moreover, when improving form, the trainer—unlike the jockey—must take the horse as it is.

That racehorses often, indeed mostly, pull therefore proves nothing. What matters here is which position of the center of gravity appears most favorable—indeed, ideal—for the racing gallop, upon calm examination of the relevant conditions.

If one considers that in the flat horse the hindquarters project far beyond the track of the forehand, so that the latter must accelerate by its own force, it can hardly appear favorable if the forehand is heavily loaded. Whatever forces in the horse may bring about elevation—opinions differ—the workload would in any case be enormous and far more taxing than if the horse loaded forehand and hindquarters approximately evenly.

Furthermore, it struck me that [James] Fillis, even for the racing gallop, does not wish to carry out any restraining influence in a backward direction (nose drawn in), but rather—even here—forward and upward (nose slightly in front). Practical experimentation confirmed the advantage of this manner most emphatically. The stride became noticeably lighter, more springy, and more pleasant; the relief of hand and loins was downright astonishing; the seat automatically went better with the horse; one could clearly feel that the forehand was relieved and the horse could move both more easily and more quickly.

Finally, I myself owned a Thoroughbred mare, small and somewhat insufficient as a horse, but—so I believe—naturally endowed with the gallop of a class horse. By nature she positioned herself exactly as Fillis recommends: the neck extended very far, but not deep—rather lightly raised—with the nose slightly in front of the vertical. She placed the rider so that the upper body aligned nearly vertically, the seat lifted lightly, all quite of itself, and she glided forward beneath him, so to speak. One had the feeling that she galloped in perfect balance, especially with the forehand, whose action was infinitely flat, almost without any knee bend, merely touching the ground. Both—the completely flat action and the almost breath-like touching of the ground—were also striking in the walk. At the same time she was extremely light in the rein, so that one almost felt one would have to drive her forward slightly rather than the opposite; very maneuverable and without any difficulty in halting. Although I have ridden Thoroughbreds exclusively for years, I have never before nor since felt anything similarly perfect in innate movement beneath me—the nose slightly in front of the vertical, so to speak flowing beneath the rider.

Anatomically speaking, I believe that balance should be regarded as by far the most favorable center-of-gravity position in the horse, even for the flat racer. In order to endure a race without fatigue, this must of course be innate. If it is, it saves seconds upon seconds, lengths upon lengths. I therefore believe that the concept of the ideal racehorse can be defined as:

"innate, flawless balance with equally flawless back mechanics."

Certainly such a horse also places its weight far forward—but not within the horse through deep lowering of the forehand; rather through broad support via wide extension of neck and head and prolonged ground contact of the hindquarters at the moment of push-off, corresponding to the enormously wide reach of the limbs as counteraction. Through this, the moment is continually found that restores the innate balance of the horse stride by stride and prevents a collapse of the forehand. That the back swings energetically, arching and lowering, follows naturally.

Despite the wide frame in which such a horse moves, its gallop is therefore not merely back movement in the crude sense, but in the highest degree—the horse is thus "collected." To speak with von Krane, it possesses "the coordination of neck and spine as well as a tendency in the gait that meets the demands imposed by tempo and gait."

And even more! Not despite but precisely because of the wide frame in which the racehorse assembles its spine, it retains both balance and freedom to continually re-assemble the strongest arching and lowering (back action). Sharper collection downward would not only worsen balance but would also hinder the immense degree of arching required here.

The implicit idea that collection for practical use can also be too narrow—when the enormous impulsion of strong gaits already fills a broader elastic frame and thereby produces back action—I would also have liked to see more sharply emphasized for the campaign horse in the author's explanations. The author nowhere directly says anything false in this regard, yet one cannot help feeling that he would wish the horse, the stronger the gait, to go ever deeper rather than simply more assembled.

On the other hand, I hold the view that a horse secure in balance performs its work with less effort and more elasticity if, when strengthening the gait, it retains the same organization and merely expands its frame inch by inch. The impulsion of the gait then nevertheless fills this frame completely.

The other method leads either to loss of balance or to that artificially assembled horse which the author presents to us at the end of the chapter in the temporarily "too deeply burdened" horse introduced as a dressage example. Pullers, in my opinion, are almost without exception artificially produced simply through excessively sharp collection.

I therefore cannot warm to these artificial shifts of the center of gravity, even of temporary nature. For a class rider, perhaps; but certainly not for hack-riding! Hand-artists will rejoice in having found a new slogan, will misunderstand the author, and will sell us a horse compressed on the forehand as his "indeed deeply burdened, but all the more stepping-under behind" horse. If a weak-backed horse adopts a similar posture under driving aids on a light hand and is released of itself—good! But with the better horse one should also allow its self-chosen posture.

Chapter Five

Purpose and Importance of the Lateral Movements in Dressage. How they are to be Executed. Conclusions for the Training.

By lateral exercises we understand here every movement in which the hindquarters and forehand—if only to a minimal degree—travel on separate paths. We therefore count among them, in addition to leg-yielding, also turning away and breaking off, since in these exercises as well the hindquarters relative to the forehand—even if only to a very small extent—are displaced from the track.

The true lateral movements in the sense of the high school we also include among them; however, we note from the outset that riders are seldom capable of maintaining the high degree of collection required for them, or of understanding how to complete the immediate return to straightness.

Without simultaneous improvement of the throughness or advancement of the horse to the point that straight work makes throughness easier for him, every exercise is completely worthless. Indeed, no exercise—whatever its name—can ever have any other purpose than to prepare, produce, or perfect throughness.

With this, we have already established the purpose of lateral exercises with which we initially intended to concern ourselves. What is especially important in this determination is first and foremost its negative aspect, namely that lateral exercises can never be an end in themselves, but are only auxiliary means for forming energetic, straight-going gaits.[36]

Their significance lies in the fact that in each of these movements the horse is forced onto a far narrower and more unstable base for balancing his own load and that of the rider than on a straight line. The horse therefore becomes far more sensitive to changes in the center of gravity; consequently, the aids can also be brought to bear far more effectively—i.e., more emphatically with a resistant horse, more finely and lightly with an obedient one.

But not only finer and lighter! Above all, more correct!

For by placing the horse into a lateral exercise, we assign him a differently configured activity of his two halves. Spine and trunk bend hollow on one side,

---

[36] *Practical note: For military riding this means chiefly that whether horses become slightly restless during their schooling or lose regularity of the steps—as one says nowadays—is entirely irrelevant. What matters solely is to push through the aids against which they resist, to force suppleness for them in calm, relaxed struggle. Success can only be recognized later, when riding straight ahead again, but then in "steps" that are energetic and regulated as if by a metronome.*

while on the other they bulge outward; one hind leg swings, the other supports more strongly; and accordingly the horse takes a fuller contact on one rein and a looser one on the other. The rider therefore feels the activity of each individual part far more clearly and distinctly than on the straight line, and is able both to determine more accurately the difficulties still opposing throughness and to apply the aids for correcting them more sensitively and at the proper moment.

Finally—and this is the most important point—the raw or unfinished horse is by nature crooked and therefore moves entirely of his own accord constantly in a certain, albeit incorrect, lateral position. We can only make this disappear through slow reshaping by means of other lateral exercises, in such a way that at any given moment we can ride the lateral exercise that we want or require.

Such a horse we call "straightened." We call it so! For, as Mr. von Oettingen once again most keenly remarks: "*There is no straight horse under the rider; we must always ride with an inner side and an outer side.*"

The aforementioned natural crookedness[37] of the horse is in itself no hindrance to throughness. Even the rawest horse, provided only that it goes forward in response to driving aids, will show throughness or will acquire it shortly, if the rider understands how to feel the natural, inborn crookedness, accommodates his seat to it, and in it pushes the horse together from behind toward the front.

The inborn defect is characterized in the average horse[38] by the fact that over its entire length it is bent concave to the right and convex to the left. The consequences appear in the neck, trunk, and hindquarters approximately as follows.

In the neck, the horse will not be inclined to set itself straight. If one leaves head position and degree of contact to him, he will retain the inborn right-hollow bend and, within it—so far as one can speak of contact in a raw horse—will seek a fairly even contact on both reins.

This will, however, remain in effect only so long as the rider behaves entirely passively and carefully avoids any change to this condition. If he does intervene, the following picture will roughly emerge: to a bending influence of the right rein the horse will willingly and without showing sensitivity follow, even if the influence is applied with a certain degree of pressure, and in doing so—entirely analogous to a ridden horse—will come more strongly toward the left. The existing concave bend to the right favors an elastic yielding, and likewise the left side does not oppose the convex bending demanded of it, since this bend is already present by nature.

---

[37] *To avoid misunderstandings, we add that naturally the horse on the straight line—of which we spoke in the preceding chapters—also possesses this imperfection. In dressage, the degree of it naturally changes. More precisely stated, by "horse on the straight line" we mean the horse with the momentarily possible degree of straightness available to him.*

[38] *In rare cases one also finds horses that are crooked in the opposite direction. For them, of course, everything applies correspondingly in reverse.*

Conversely, a bending influence of the left rein will be unsympathetic to the horse. If the influence reaches a certain strength, the horse will express his sensitivity through head tossing and similar signs. Only a very delicate, merely suggestive rein aid may perhaps be tolerated. He will neither yield elastically on the left rein nor come more strongly to the right rein. Instead, the influence merely presses the convex neck muscles together without result and causes the horse discomfort—indeed pain—and this not only directly on the left, but also on the right concave side, which is unaccustomed to convex bending.

If, on the other hand, the horse is prevented from assuming his inborn posture by the rider's straightening hand, then—if he submits at all—he will feel stiff, indeed hard, on the left and loose on the right. I shall return to this in greater detail in Chapter Six.

The natural bend continues into the trunk. The horse presses the ribs outward to the left and demands a correspondingly shifted rider's seat if he is to remain free and unrestrained in his natural condition.

Finally, the sphere of movement of the hind legs must also, as a consequence of this displacement of the trunk, shift leftward to serve as support for the load. The hind feet therefore do not step exactly toward the forehand; the right steps more toward the horse's midline, the left slightly outward away from the body.[39] From this results the well-known aversion—escalating in some horses to the most extreme resistance—to obeying the left leg.

From these natural conditions we must seek to derive both the justification for lateral movements as well as the conditions for their correct gymnastic execution.

We find the crooked gait, although the horse, as mentioned, is soft and can be ridden as a back-walker with the necessary skill of the rider, even in him. A trained racehorse is soft and a back-walker, but only rarely straightened—chiefly for two reasons he is not burdened with this. First, the horse never fully uses his strength, because the hind leg, which is positioned away from the horse's body, always loses part of its thrust, since it does not strike the body directly from behind; secondly, true mastery of the horse by the rider[40] is unthinkable.

We do not wish to dwell on the first point, which has caused the ruin of so many horses, where rein-lameness plays a major role and never allows the horse true mastery over his own body; rather, we wish to linger on the second point

---

[39] *I know very well that the opposite view is the commonly held one: that when one brings the horse in front, this naturally has its effect on the hindquarters. We also found for rein contact that bringing the horse in front represents a complete reversal of natural conditions; the horse is fixed in front on the left, appears to come better to the right, while—left in his inborn crookedness—he is sensitive to the influence of that rein and evades it. Chapter VI treats these questions more thoroughly.*

[40] *In military riding, the back-walking tendency would also be quickly lost; for only very few riders are capable of riding a pronouncedly crooked horse through. Yet even they cannot truly master a crooked horse.*

in order to learn the natural conditions for mastering the horse more precisely than has been done so far.

Only briefly shall we indicate it. In the second point lies the main matter.

A primary requirement for mastery of the horse is, first of all, to be able to stop a horse that has been brought into a fast gait with propriety, with preservation of the legs, and with appropriate promptness.

Let us assume that horse and rider together represent a weight of 1,000 to 1,400 pounds; then the unnaturalness of the idea of wanting to stop this mass—whose living force, in full motion, could rise to many metric tons—with the hand becomes so obvious that one should never even come upon the idea of attempting such a thing.

On the contrary!

But practice unfortunately teaches all too often the opposite.

Naturally, the shortening of the gait can occur only when something similar counters the weight rolling forward.

If the horse has learned in dressage to place his hindquarters far underneath himself in response to a light aid, then one needs only to request this in order to cause the combined weight of horse and rider to sink significantly backward.

The horse thus produces for himself a restraining aid whose mechanical effect can, through the rider's backward inclination, substantially increase the rider's weight by his own initiative.

At the same time, the muscles of the hindquarters bracing against the ground—which become powerfully tensioned through the far-reaching stepping-under—draw, by means of the back muscles, the forehand toward themselves and thereby newly inhibit the forward movement, without the rein playing any role other than a merely indicative one.

For dressage, this explanation of the half-halt, which in itself is not new but is often disregarded—as thousands of examples in arena and terrain demonstrate—is extremely important.

For even here, though to a lesser degree, this continual stepping-under of the hindquarters through the driving aids, the springy loading of the stepped-under hind leg through the rider's weight, and the resulting muscular pull give us that chain of effects by which the activity of the hand is rendered superfluous, the horse is led to true collection, and is thereby enabled later, even in practice at full speed, willingly to step the hindquarters under in order to make use of the "natural" forces for the halt.

In this process we are, of course, to some extent dependent upon the good will of the horse; yet the obedience rooted through frequent habit in dressage to the flashing spur will not fail even under partial resistance, as a sharp "halt and stand!" has already brought many a mutineer to reason.

Only one thing could become dangerous for us: namely, if the horse were also to resist at the other end of the spring with which we have so frequently compared him—by boring forward with the poll and thereby drawing the muscles of back and hindquarters toward it, in order thus to evade the backward shift of weight.

The crooked horse would be particularly well suited to this; for the inborn convexity of the left side of the neck increases the more the muscles are compressed together. Even in moderate collection we find here an outwardly bulging swelling; the entire musculature and tendons, indeed even the vertebrae themselves, press outward.

This convex curvature, which also exists in the ribs, is now integrated into the connection bridle–hind hoof, and here, too, we are confronted with a physical law according to which the convex form of a springing object makes the approximation of its two ends more difficult, while the concave form facilitates it.

From this follows the demand that the neck be bent concavely close behind the poll. Only in this form do we have the guarantee that the supple stepping-under of the corresponding hind leg translates into a hollow bending of the entire horse up to the poll, thereby producing thrust-off and yielding into the softly counter-tensioning hand.

We must therefore be able, in dressage, to bend each side concavely, in order to be able to counter-bend against it in an emergency. Under no circumstances, however, may we permit the horse to retain the hardened convex bulging of the raw neck musculature, which would place a premium upon opposition.

Furthermore, every rider[41] will surely have noticed how helpless one stands opposite a crooked horse when it wants to break out to the left or make a left turn. The convex bending of the left side allows the horse at any moment to press against the rein of that side or to throw itself completely around.

Just as little can the right rein exert a restraining effect; for the time being it possesses only a bending effect, which is more suited to promoting the pressing of the forehand to the left than to inhibiting it.

One may say briefly: neither left shoulder-in aids nor left travers aids—with which one most readily nails down a horse breaking out to the left or most securely suppresses a left volte—are accepted by the horse.

Thus, if we wish to intervene against bolting, rearing, or breaking out—the three forms of disobedience that most frequently appear in practical use—we must first ensure that the horse is straightened through lateral movements.

Let us therefore ask about the natural conditions, first, for the choice of the correct lateral movements, and secondly, for their correct execution.

One thing becomes clear at first glance: namely, that the previously popular practice of bending horses from the outset to the right and left, breaking them out, etc., can scarcely be correct—even if it is said that one should work more on

---

[41] *Naturally only the good rider feels the lack of suppleness. The great majority of riders would call such a horse "mean, nervous, fearful," etc.; in truth, it is merely stiff and untrained.*

the stiff side. A merely quantitative difference will not suffice here; it must be a qualitative one!

The most natural thing would be to say: we must make our horse obedient to the left rein and leg, achieve hollow bending on that side—in short, always ride the horse with left shoulder-in aids—then it will gradually become straight.

This left hollow-bending is unquestionably the goal toward which we must arrive (as we shall later see, the highest task for the horse under discussion is right travers in correct, supple form; but this is attainable only via left shoulder-in). Yet an immediate beginning with left shoulder-in work is, precisely by outstanding riders (e.g., by Mr. von Reudell),[42] recommended in a manner that seems convincing.

Here I represent exactly the opposite view.

Mr. von Reudell proceeds here from the principle: *"What I can take hold of, I can also work,"* and continues: *"The horse does not stand on the right, but on the left rein alone."*

This is by no means correct. As we have already indicated and shall later prove more precisely, this applies only when we force our hand upon the horse, compelling it to stand straight ahead or even to the left. And even then only the first part is correct; the second is not.

Rather, a horse that is behind the right rein becomes hard and unsupple toward the other[43] and resists—if with difficulty—its demands to the point of despair.

The recommended method of "taking hold" is therefore suitable only for masters of the art, who truly "can take hold"—that is, who, conscious of their superiority over the horse, need not fear directly provoking resistance.

Yet even of this applies what we had to say with regard to the bitting system of Plinzner in the footnote on page 17: comfortably and effortlessly even the best rider does not work, nor does the best-built horse form itself, by this method.

In any case, natural horsemanship cannot follow this direct, sharply grasping path. For its essence lies precisely in the fact that it does not take as its starting point what should be, but rather that we begin with exactly the same horse exactly as it is.

---

[42] *In the first edition, I appeared to follow Herr von Reudell; however, neither with him nor with me did this actually take place. The explanation lay in the assertion that one must begin on the left only with raw horses, with the explicit addition: "ridden horses do not come into consideration here." Since nowadays truly raw horses scarcely come into the hand, I believed that this was the reason why the right side appeared to me as the starting side for most horses—that is, that in substance we were in agreement. Thus I would begin on a raw horse likewise on the left, but on my ridden horse likewise on the right. I have since convinced myself that this is not the case.*

[43] *The analogous thought seems to me to be expressed by Herr Kurt von Tepper-Laski [wrote in the equestrian book titled] "Rennreiten: Praktische Winke für Rennreiter und Manager" [Horse Racing: Practical Tips for Jockeys and Managers] thus: "As paradoxical as it may sound to the layman, the effect of the rein does not lie in the reins."*

It takes the inborn condition of the horse as its working basis and gradually transforms it—like the rising moon, which ascends imperceptibly and yet in relatively short time reaches the zenith.

One should never want everything at once in life; and as everywhere else, so especially in dressage the greatest detours are often the shortest paths to the goal.

We therefore consider another procedure to be indicated.

We have already mentioned that a raw horse, despite its crookedness, can be ridden entirely as a back-walker if one accommodates oneself to it with one's seat. The advantages of influencing a back-walker are, however, so immeasurably great (compare chapters one and three) that we cannot forgo them.

We therefore ask ourselves: which lateral movement will disturb our horse's back-walking the least? Which most closely resembles the horse's inborn fault?

Undoubtedly the latter is a corrupted right shoulder-in. The horse deviates with the hindquarters to the left, but does not swing forward with the outer hind leg; instead, it places it downward along its body, from which arises the deficient approach to the left rein.

For we must establish this: from the counter-swinging of the hindquarters against the reins arises their tension and thus their self-acting effect.

If we now encourage the horse, while maintaining its inborn crooked position, with both legs—primarily the right, which it will more willingly accept, since it does not oppose the horse's fault—to increased forward movement, it will strive forward; but if we suppress this striving, after some time the horse will push itself off to the right and thereby come toward the left rein.

At the same time it will shift even more with the hindquarters to the left and run of its own accord into the left leg.

Both will succeed all the more easily because the entire load of the horse, by virtue of its right shoulder-in positioning, swings from right to left and thus quasi runs into the left aids.

If we now repeatedly continue forward riding and allowing the right push-off through tensioning of the croup and right hand, we obtain the right rein ever more lightly, the left ever fuller in the hand, until we finally have the horse—though still crooked in relation to its direction of movement—evenly on both reins.

But the effect also proceeds here, and we wish to emphasize this again, from the hindquarters.

For if we ask what the left hind leg has done in the meantime, we see that it initially stepped downward away from the horse's body. We could not prevent this, because the loose left rein was not in a position to offer resistance to the swing of the hind leg; nor did we wish to prevent it, in order not to disturb the horse's running into the left leg, the self-initiated request for this aid on the part of the horse.

But the more the horse pressed against the outer aids, the less these yielded, until finally a true resisting of them developed, and from this a driving forward with the leg and a receiving resistance with the hand.

The driving into the left hand increases more and more the fuller the rein, which is constantly becoming fuller, gives room to the swing.

The left hind leg can brace itself against it, and finally the left hind leg steps forward with swing, just like the right one, in the right shoulder-in positioning. The horse thus enters, as it were, a well-collected haunches-in; both hind legs swing off energetically, both reins have elastic contact.

If the driving of the left leg is increased, opposing the left side and even carried beyond this point, then the left hind leg will increasingly and finally more than the right step under, thereby hollow-bending the entire left side and thus also acting on the neck, and after a certain time we shall see this produce a kind of *renvers*.[44]

We shall, however, regretfully observe that the innate outward evasion of the left hind leg is again and again sought after from time to time. If the left leg is not very attentive, here and there the left hind leg will again fall out.

To punish our willing horse for these small mishaps by reverting to the old fault would be harsh and unjust. We must therefore devise a means to correct this calmly and with composure.

Our horse is again, after some practice, in the renvers-like gait, bent well to the left. Should it now resist the demand, for example to turn left on about one-sixth of a volte, and thereby assume the counter-shoulder-in position, the situation is exactly the same, only the direction of movement changes. For the bend of the horse remains the same.

The horse has thereby unknowingly gone into a trap, for this apparently so harmless change of the direction of movement of its body from left to right is very significant. The left hind leg can no longer step outward; rather it can only resist the leg aid (and then the spur comes—soft, but relentless), or it must now step toward the middle of the horse, that is, under its own and the rider's weight.

Through this salutary exercise the left hind leg gains ever more suppleness, and after some time a minimum of left leg suffices to maintain left shoulder-in position.

---

[44] *In the text, in order not to interrupt the flow of the exposition, the development is carried out on one hand, the right. Therefore, we follow the transformation of the horse from right shoulder-in, through renvers [haunches-out], to counter-shoulder-in, to travers [haunches-in]. In practice, however, it would be better if we begin [tracking left] with left shoulder-in, proceed to left travers [haunches-in], followed by counter-shoulder-in to the right and travers to the right. Bend and positioning relative to the direction of movement of the horse thus remain the same as above. For the large horse as well as for the average rider, however, the initial bends in counter-shoulder-in/travers are easier than in shoulder-in/renvers. Later, the latter will then also succeed more readily.*

We increase the exercise more and more, but our horse is not only willing but also clever. It will soon feel that it can spare the left hind leg even in this position. To do so it needs only to let the right hind leg step downward away from the horse's body and to place the left hind leg, instead of stepping over that one, next to it, in order to escape the unsympathetic bending.

But we, too, do not sleep.

We have accustomed ourselves to seek the essence of the lateral movement not in the movement itself, but in the manner and way in which it is ridden.

While maintaining left shoulder-in position, we now draw the right hind leg nearer and nearer with the corresponding leg, prevent its falling out, and thus force the left hind leg to step diagonally over the right, thereby strongly bending.

As the load now swings from left to right and the right leg drives ever more powerfully forward, the right rein will become fuller and fuller: *"we shall finally be forced to brace against it."*

As always, after a short time the counter-swinging of the horse against the steady, softly yielding hand will translate into a pushing-off from it. Then, however, the right hind leg, which we have unceasingly improved, will step underneath more easily, more comfortably, and ever more. It will finally do this to such a degree that it acts hollow-bending upon the entire right side of the horse—and before we are aware of it, the horse has set us bent to the right and goes of its own accord—right *travers*.

This repositioning of our own person—this only now becomes clear to us—has already been carried out by the horse twice: from right shoulder-in to left travers, from that to left shoulder-in, together with us; we simply did not pay attention to it, because we, accustomed always to accommodate ourselves with the seat to the horse obedient to the aids, to enter into its movement, also yielded ourselves to the horse in the lateral lessons.

And now we also realize that we natural riders, without thinking anything special about it, have in fact ridden the lateral movements—which most authors present as the most mystical and artful element of the high school—albeit in far lesser collection. How? When we make use, on the so-called straight line, of the acquired suppleness of the hind legs, the permeability of ribs, haunches, and poll—in short, the higher capacity for collection of the entire horse—in order to bring the horse on this line into a willingly offered higher collection; when this has become easy for the horse, we repeat the unconsciously ridden cycle of lateral movements in higher collection, then once again increase the collection on the straight line, and so on—would we then not, one fine day, truly be able to ride highly collected lateral movements?

Certainly—but we shall not do so, because for our practical purposes lateral movements in such high collection are entirely unnecessary.

Yet for our practical purposes we nevertheless learn an enormous amount from this realization!

Purpose and Importance of the Lateral Movements

First, we now understand the value and significance which the old high school attributed to true lateral movements. They were not even there an end in themselves! Rather, they were for the old masters entirely natural performances of the horse, when one guided it into a collection with so far-back-lying a center of gravity as was the case then, while at the same time keeping the horse as permeable as is necessary for the suppleness and impulsion of the gaits straight ahead.

A horse that truly goes softly and permeably in Spanish walk must, in haunches, ribs, and poll, also be so thoroughly laterally supple that it is capable of executing the lateral movements in the sense of the high school faultlessly. If it cannot do these, then hardness will also be present in Spanish walk at this or that point.

They have the same significance even today. The whole difference is that we no longer strive for a collection with such a far-back-lying center of gravity.

Within the collection that we desire, however, a truly through-ridden horse must still today be just as permeable to right and left leg, right and left rein, that it can perform the lateral movements in this collection. If this is impossible, then the gaits on the straight line are also not truly soft; the horse is not permeable to all aids.

Yet this has above all historical value!

For practical riding we draw far more valuable conclusions from the manner in which we brought our horse—shy of right-travers aids—up to them, first making them accessible, then making the horse permeable.

First it becomes apparent that it does not correspond to the nature of the horse to practice the lessons of right and left bending, yielding, and leg-yielding arbitrarily alternating.

In every dressage moment there is rather only one rein from which we must let the horse push off, only one leg which we must apply more strongly, only one positioning of the hindquarters to the forehand in which we must place the horse, in order to work it with true advantage. For the horse has only one difficulty, which we eliminate in the described manner through smooth transition from right shoulder-in via left travers to left shoulder-in to riding in a right-travers-like manner.

In each individual dressage moment the form in which the difficulty confronts us is a different one; the difficulty itself always remains the same—the innate asymmetrical muscular constitution of the horse. All of this is actually already contained in the sentence: *"Always work the whole horse!"*

We see secondly that working with one-sided aids is nonsense. Rather, it can only be a matter of working predominantly with one-sided aids even in the first introductions, while carefully leaving all other aids on the horse, i.e., as soon as a glimmer of possibility presents itself, also becoming active with them and, if necessary, reinforcing the predominant ones.

First, the collection which the horse already has can only be maintained with bilateral aids. But we cannot dispense with them even for the lateral lessons themselves!

For, as we have seen, the horse is forced to step over with one hind leg over the other only when the latter is held. Otherwise the horse first places it sideways and drags the other stiff and unbent behind. But the entire work, the entire bending of the one, more strongly engaging hind leg lies in stepping under the load of horse and rider, with which the horse, as it were, has to play ball.

It is exactly the same with the reins! As soon as the horse yields to one rein, pushes itself off from it, the other must laterally stabilize the neck through counter-tension, or else it slides outward along its entire length and the bending at the single decisive point—the poll—is avoided.

This too is actually already contained in the sentence:

"Always work the whole horse!"

We see thirdly how, in sensitive riding, the aids that often appear so complicated actually always remain the same extremely simple ones and merely, through the growing suppleness of the horse toward them, change from driving to bending, from working toward the rein to yielding at the rein, and thus from inside to outside and again from outside to inside.

Our horse was brought, through continuous hollow-bending to the right, up to the left rein; this rein held, became fuller and fuller. At the same time the horse increasingly went into the left leg, which at first did not drive against it only because the left rein was not yet strong enough in the hand to hold counter to any thrust of the corresponding hind leg.

As soon as feel confirmed this possibility, the rider drove forward, made the left rein still fuller, at the same time increasingly restricted the swinging of the hindquarters, until the left hind foot stepped equally with the right in the positioning of right shoulder-in.

If the horse was then driven still more forward, the previously outer hind foot became inner, shifted the rider, bent itself more, brought left bend into the entire horse, and caused yielding from the left rein. For all true yielding is nothing other than the natural consequence of increased stepping under of the hindquarters, or predominantly of one hind foot.

The connection between hind hoof and bit thus becomes shorter[45] on the inner, concave side, longer on the outer, convex side as soon as the horse bends hollow: the same occurs on the so-called straight line for the direction from back to front. If a horse steps under with the hindquarters while the hand remains soft in its place, the reins become looser because the horse itself has become shorter, while the length of the connection "bit–rein" remains the same.

---

[45] *On the so-called straight line the same occurs for the direction from back to front. If a horse steps under with the hindquarters while the hand remains softly in its place, the reins become looser because the horse itself becomes shorter, while the length of the connection "bit–rein" remains unchanged.*

Purpose and Importance of the Lateral Movements

With a floating hand, therefore, the outer rein must, itself become fuller, the inner looser.

Here too the necessity becomes apparent never to forget: *"Always work the whole horse!"*

We see fourthly the great simplicity of the basic principle in all apparent complications. As soon as the horse accepts the left aids, the entire wisdom for practice resolves into the simple instruction:

"Always keep the horse driven up to both reins with both legs; now feel toward which leg, toward which rein your horse tends more, then drive more with that one and thereby also induce the hand to hold more strongly against it."

This too means nothing other than: *"Always work the whole horse!"*

We see fifthly what role the seat plays, although we have scarcely spoken a single word about it so far. We omitted it because leg aids are more familiar to everyone precisely for the lateral lessons and in fact here still come more into supporting effect than on the so-called straight line. Moreover, a special chapter is to be devoted to the doctrine of the aids on the bent horse.

But: who held the horse in the changing positioning to the point of impact? Who maintained the swing of the back? Who created the decisive difference between right shoulder-in and left travers, or later left shoulder-in and right travers at the moment when both hind feet step under evenly in the right (or left) positioning?—Only the seat, which softly accommodates itself to the correctly fitting center of gravity of the horse entering into the lateral lesson, yields to it, allows itself to be carried by the horse itself, but just as softly resists the incorrectly placed center of gravity of the horse and through its quiet activity irresistibly forces it into the correct relationships.

If it is wrong, unstable, or lacking suppleness, then farewell harmony of movement between rider and horse, rider's feel, softness, swing of the back!

Nowhere does the feeling rider sense the infinite power of the seat as much as in the lateral lessons—but unfortunately also, in a sense, its mystery, since its effect is exercised instinctively, unconsciously, and is anticipated by the rider who, relaxing from the thigh in seat and leg, feels every oscillation of the horse's weight with his own weight, yet resists intellectual analysis—even after years of painstaking observation.

Here the saying truly applies: *"Everything lies in the seat!"*

We see sixthly how all lateral lessons—bending, yielding, leg-yielding, and the lateral movements—are fundamentally the same lessons and differ only by the degree of collection, which in the beginning of dressage can only be slight, but in the course of training becomes ever higher.

The horse capable only of slight collection will first bend when ridden forward in right shoulder-in position, because the elongated neck allows greater bending.

If later, with higher collection, the neck is closely compressed, bending will quite of itself have become shoulder-in, because the neck in this tight position no longer permits large lateral bending.

Likewise, when the horse makes the first approach to left travers, it will be broken off with the left hind foot just beginning to step under more; the more it later steps under with the left hind foot, learns to hollow-bend the left side, the more it will approach true travers.

Likewise, in (e.g. left) leg-yielding, left shoulder-in, left renvers or right counter-shoulder-in, and right travers are all completely contained in their beginnings.

Here too the difference lies solely in the higher or lower degree of collection possible for the horse at the moment. The horse that still goes long and low will yield to the leg; the one already accessible to tighter collection will go one of the lateral movements—remembering that correct collection, as already explained above, always contains within itself the possibility of allowing either hind leg to swing or carry more.

This too, is in itself not new. But if we look around the riding arenas, one might think this inner connection were clear to only a few.

Instead of every horse in a riding section performing the lateral lessons in the highest degree of collection specifically possible for it—and thus quite naturally, for example, yielding to the leg, or placing the forehand on the track, or going shoulder-in, without any sharply delimited transition between these three stages of one and the same lesson becoming perceptible—we often hear for horses in good collection the commands: *"Horses bend right," "Yield to the right leg,"* etc.; for horses of every outline still only from a certain moment onward the commands: *"Shoulder-in," "Travers,"* etc.

Both are schematic forms of work, with disregard for the unity of all these lateral movements.

Both are harmful! In the one case it is pointless to work a horse at a lower degree of collection than is possible for him, unless perhaps the experienced rider, after several days of very sharp work that excites the horse's nerves, wishes, with well-considered intention, to give light work as an exception. In the other case, the foundation of dressage is undermined when riders are tempted, by demands for performances that are still impossible for the horse at that time, to resort to exaggerated aids, in which, naturally, recourse is taken first of all to the rein.

Moreover, one not only ruins this rider, but also destroys in him the rider sensitive feeling. It is not considered good riding to allow a neck to hang long that willingly collapses under driving, or to allow a hindquarter to be flung outward, when we are able to hold it effortlessly.

On the contrary, we must educate our riders up to instinctive execution, so that in every movement, whatever its name may be, they always push the hindquarters as much as is ever possible against the passive hand. Otherwise we will never attain that totality of driving aids which is necessary for the reshaping of truly unfavorable conformations and for the development of genuinely swinging gaits.

Dressage is simply not a pleasure ride, and only under a rider who continuously, unconsciously, and to the highest permissible degree pushes his horse forward before him with driving aids can the phrase *"Always work the whole horse"* become reality.[46]

For only through such a rider is the second focal point of all riding wisdom—*"Everything lies in the seat!"*—brought into practical effectiveness. With most riders, both truths remain empty phrases due to a lack of driving aids.

After all this, it might appear as though we were enthusiastic friends of lateral movements. We are by no means so—at least not for the time being! Only the rider just described, for whom working and driving have become identical concepts, may ride across the arena with impunity. Nowhere is it more important to ride forward at the same time than when riding laterally.

Nevertheless, our remarks are also of significance for the rider to whom lateral movements are not permitted. For even on the so-called straight line, as we have seen, the horse goes in an incorrect lateral movement, going more against one leg or one rein.

If, as an instructor, one allows riders to drive continually more with that leg and to resist more with that rein, without allowing the opposing aids to let the horse go, one will still always achieve quite good—indeed much better—results than if one allows riders, without giving them anything to think about, to turn by throwing away the outside rein and to let the horse evade the other by means of a blocked or dead (so-called "guarding," but in fact unfortunately almost always dead) outside leg.

If one at the same time takes the trouble to make the nature of the crookedness clear to the riders, brings them to relaxation in hips, knees, and legs—upon which, above all, the rider's tactful feeling, such as driving with the seat, depends—then they will gradually learn to feel, precisely through the constant use of the aids which the horse accepts and against which he goes,[47]

---

[46] *We cannot refrain from emphasizing once again at this point that only this manner of riding corresponds to the nature of the horse. Every driving aid, by natural necessity, goes through the entire horse, because the horse's natural impulse urges him to balance the load placed on the hindquarters by the driving forward, thereby calling forth the effect of the rein and thus continually restoring the elastic tension between hindquarters and forehand. With the rein aid, the matter is the reverse. In itself, of its own accord, it never goes through the entire horse; rather, it only does so when the good rider instinctively pushes the hindquarters correspondingly forward at the same time. In itself alone, it runs contrary to the natural impulse of the horse to go forward again under load.*

[47] *"Accepting the aids" and "going against the aids" are, in correct riding, identical concepts; in incorrect riding, of course, they are opposites. In the first case the horse goes elastically; in the latter, inelastically, hard against the aids. Closely connected with this is the hard and the soft side of the horse. Here perhaps lies the most decisive moment for the entire art of riding. We shall therefore treat this question in a separate chapter. Between the lines, however, the answer is already given in this chapter.*

especially since even the simplest understanding must grasp that the more successfully one enforces these aids, the more the horse must become permeable to them and thus obedient.

Editor's Closing Word

The author treats something entirely new here. Neither von Krane nor the *Riding Instruction*, neither the system of Plinzner[48] nor Fillis go beyond a more or less superficial consideration of the crookedness of the "horse," whereas the author finds in it, both theoretically and above all practically, precisely the foundation for correct muscular formation and through-ness.

In order to recognize this in its full scope, however, a small gap in the chain of proof must still be filled. To demonstrate the importance of correct use of crookedness, the author says only the following:

"We have already mentioned that a horse, despite his crookedness, can be ridden entirely as a back-mover if one accommodates oneself to him with one's seat. However, the advantages of influence upon a back-mover are so immeasurably great (see chapters one and three) that we cannot possibly forgo them."

For full clarity regarding the significance of his idea, two things are missing here:
1. the inversion of this statement, and
2. the reference to that advantage of back-movement which is especially the most important for the formation of the musculature.

If we take up the latter first, the following would have to be explained:

What comes into consideration here above all is the elastic counter-springing of the musculature of hindquarters and forehand that is eo ipso present in the back-mover. This brings it about that every stepping under of the hind legs, or of one of them, via the haunch-pelvis-back muscles, draws the muscles of the forehand toward itself and thereby slightly relaxes the elastic tension for a moment, only to strengthen it again just as easily in the next moment through the push-off, and so on.[49]

In a word: even the crooked horse is soft of himself, and not merely on one, but on both reins, provided only that the rider does not obstruct the longer path of the convexly arched muscles of the naturally bent side during the oscillation back and forth, and likewise allows the shorter path of the concavely compressed muscles of the naturally hollow side.

If he regards this crooked position as the one that is "straight for this horse," then after riding around the arena two or three times—whereby the crooked position naturally remains exactly the same whether he is on the right or left

---

[48] With regard to the Plinzner system, compare the concluding paragraph of the "Wochenblatt" [Weekly Bulletin] article printed in Chapter Eight from No. 56, 1900.

[49] This is the true meaning of the previously good riding expression: "The horse is on the rein." Or: A horse is on the rein when, at every step, every jump, in the moment of suspension, an atom goes toward the rein by means of the musculature of back and hindquarters acting here in a drawing, there in a pushing manner upon the forehand.

rein—he will bring the completely undisturbed, swinging horse to harmless letting-go and see it approach all aids, right as well as left, with confidence.[50]

It will then insert both—naturally slightly oblique toward the spine—seat aids, with both—naturally likewise slightly correspondingly displaced—legs into both—naturally slightly differently long—reins; in short, it will willingly compress itself upon driving aids. With full skill on the part of the rider, the horse is for the direction from behind to in front just as permeable as a finished horse; the swing encounters nowhere on the path from the hindquarters to the bit any friction, inhibition, or interruption.

"He goes back and forth so smoothly and sucking-like as in a well-cleaned machine, the piston in its cylinder."

(As editor I add: *"The machine merely needs to be oiled; the horse merely needs to be made laterally supple."*)

To illuminate the reverse side, one could continue as follows:

All this occurs, as stated, only when the innate crookedness is fully felt and seat as well as hand completely accommodate themselves to it. Already when riding straight ahead, every attempt—even the most cautious—to straighten the horse from the front more or less interrupts or at least disturbs the back-movement. But if the rider works in the arena and believes that on the right rein he can or must place his horse to the right, and on the left rein to the left, then *"he begins the training of the horse with a complete interruption of back-movement."*

The swing of the hindquarters finds on its path toward the forehand—whether in haunch, back, or neck musculature—with most riders unfortunately resistance, friction, and inhibition at all these points.

Then the horse resembles a machine that not only remains un-oiled, but is disturbed in its operation by grains of sand, dirt, or even bending of the piston.

If these disturbances reach a certain degree, the machine, despite the most perfect construction, can no longer continue working—and the same applies to the best, most swinging horse. Beyond a certain limit it can no longer swing through, just as little as a bent piston can continue to go back and forth smoothly in its cylinder.

The horse can be compared to a machine only in a very limited sense. It is, after all, also a living creature with nerves and sensations of pain! The latter already arise—designated as "constraint"—even with the finest and best rider, as soon as antagonistic springs press ever more tightly together, forcing the muscles gradually into a cramped compression. How much more so, then, when the ordinary average rider from the outset places a horse—one that by nature would carry its nose four inches to the right—one inch to the left!?

---

[50] *This conception goes a trifle further than that expressed by the author. He had the same idea. Only to him, as is understandable, the handling of the exceedingly difficult, until then entirely neglected question did not fully succeed. I shall return to this later.*

In short, let us make this brief: within ten minutes the rider is seated on a pronounced crooked-goer.

The horse, out of natural necessity, in order to avoid pain wherever it may manifest, either suppresses the impulsion from the hindquarters altogether: "It behaves!" Or else it is forced into impulsion by the better rider through energetic driving—yet then it prevents that impulsion from passing through to the endangered place: "It stiffens itself, braces itself!"

I believe that this consideration brings clearly into relief both the necessity of carefully taking the horse's crookedness into account in dressage, and the sharp contrast in which such dressage stands to today's methods. For out of 100 riders, at least 99 place their horse straight on the right rein and straight on the left rein, thereby transforming an animal prepared by nature for elastic movement into a hard, unnatural body inaccessible to the aids.

Moreover, a second point does not yet stand out sharply enough: namely, that crookedness asserts itself anew with every increase of collection, and indeed with every heightened demand—thus also especially in the canter. The horse must therefore likewise be made permeable and obedient to the aids again and again in an analogous manner.

Perhaps this requirement can best be justified for the canter if I briefly explain how I came at all to the theory of the horse's crookedness.

It too originates from the racetrack.

That horses in every gait push laterally against the rider's aids, now toward one side, now toward the other, had long been known to me. I had also long held the positive feeling that the chief secret of riding must lie in the solution of this question. Yet the inner connection remained puzzling to me.

Above all, I could not understand how a good jockey could keep a strongly pulling horse relatively permeable.

Then in 1888 in Frankfurt am Main—I believe it was Deserter under Ustable—I saw a horse execute the quite sharp left turn at the saddle place in the following manner: right lead canter, sharp left flexion; in short, counter-canter at racing pace with sharp counter-flexion toward the direction of travel. The left rein was relatively loose, while the right was sharply tensioned; the nose, in the rhythm of the stride, alternately assumed a less sharp but still very pronounced left flexion, then rebounded back into the former strikingly strong left flexion.

Yet the canter was so full of swing, the posture of the horse so natural and unconstrained, the elastic yielding before the hand so unmistakable, that the rider's cross was evidently scarcely burdened; rider and horse—felt so well in this strong yet elastic frame, despite the form being directly impossible for our dressage concepts, that the turn executed itself so smoothly that the assumed posture forced itself upon one as the only correct one for the given situation.

And suddenly it became clear to me that not despite, but precisely because of this posture, the impulsion of the hindquarters penetrated through to the forehand and thereby maintained permeability.

Further reflection on the inner connection then led, by natural necessity, to the theory presented by the author in chapter five.

When riding spoiled horses, I then made the observation that the same also allowed a practically[51] astonishingly rapid correction, especially when applied in the canter.

If, with a spoiled horse, one thinks absolutely not of the officially correct canter bend, but solely of making it permeable everywhere with seat, spur, and hand—continually pressing it with the aids it resists into the opposite ones—then the most marvelous combinations arise from the actual canter bend and the bends which the horse assumes partly in obedient yielding to the aids, partly as a consequence of clumsiness in following them as quickly as demanded.

Let us assume, for example, that we ride counter-canter on the left rein, which for horses that have become dull always offers the quickest correction, and initially in the comfortable *renvers* position. The horse follows. We then increase to a light counter shoulder-in position (relative to the track). At the moment of the transition, the horse wants to abandon the rib bend and presses inward (to the right). As a counter-aid, we shift the hindquarters one to two inches perhaps farther to the left than normal. At the same moment the horse throws itself onto the left rein, and we sharply rebuff the attack by bending left against and simultaneously steering laterally to the right, in order to demand right bend again in the next instant.

I believe it would be a prize problem for pure theoreticians to trace the approaches to the various bends that may arise here in the space of perhaps 1½ seconds, yet must always already make room for a newly emerging place, and to determine the final result.

That this lightning-fast alternation of the aids requires a certain skill on the rider's part is true; but precisely through riding under constant utilization of crookedness, one acquires it. Every rider with a supple seat gains it entirely on his own once he has grasped that only the seat—which alone can maintain the simultaneously required collection during the lateral actions—can mediate this refinement of feeling. As soon as the weights of rider and horse have truly become one in movement, the soft seat anticipates every movement of the horse.

---

[51] *This is the great advantage of all principles taken from the racetrack: that they have practical significance under all circumstances; at high speed, with full unleashing of the horse's forces, no artifice helps—only pure nature brings success. Hence also the importance of the weight aids! Every theory that takes rein action as its primary basis collapses as soon as it attempts to explain the processes on the racetrack. A theory that takes the weight aids as its point of departure explains every process there as everywhere else. If one assigns to every pound acting on a horse a pound—or a gram—a counterforce, then one has the aids of racing riding as well as of the high school.*

It alone is the true master of the horse.

If we compare the subtlety of the aids and their lightning-fast alternating sequence, it appears like a good dancing couple. The analogous situation would be as follows: At the moment when a change from right to left is initiated, a collision threatens in the execution; the right waltz must therefore be maintained, but at the same instant another couple blocks the path, and yielding backward avoids the collision threatened from both sides. Here too, separate yet in motion united weights shift within a second perhaps from right to left, from left to right, and from this movement backward—without the eye of the spectator or the dancers' own feeling perceiving any disturbance. Without balance nothing is possible; with it everything is achievable.

One does not apply the doctrine of crookedness only to spoiled horses, but with advantage to every training, particularly in the canter.

The canter admittedly already has over the trot the great advantage that the hindquarters always act as a whole, not merely one hind leg stepping under the forehand. The horse can never brace itself as strongly as in the trot; errors also become more perceptible to the rider and instructor. This benefits both the improvement of balance and of permeability. A certain degree—especially of permeability—is more easily visible and more securely attainable in the canter than in the trot.

Beyond that, slight deviations are harder to perceive in it, and precisely for their correction it is advisable to test the horse continuously for its crookedness in the canter. Nothing heightens one's own feeling as much, nor as quickly as possible, as a run on the piano executed at speed: the lateral loosening of the spinal column with a series of the lateral movement attenuations described in chapter five. The attenuation for the eye is here admittedly so great that even the observer, with strained attention, sees hardly anything of it. The aids are given by the rider so strongly, and observed by the horse so finely, that within two to three strides the cycle is completed.

Most appropriate to the canter is the sequence:

"Counter shoulder-in – Travers – Shoulder-in – Renvers," whereby the latter is either used for the change or appears as an immediately renewed counter shoulder-in as a gliding, breath-like transition. The entire process plays itself out, so to speak, inwardly between rider and horse.

For example: right rein canter! A minimal pressing of the left seat bone inward, firm tension of the corresponding rein, and pressing drive bring the horse almost imperceptibly into the right aids (counter shoulder-in); the rein fingers vibrate, the right seat bone swings the received central weight outward to generate travers; left seat bone and the forehand, using the restrained soft pressure of the outer rein, push the forehand inward as if working on a very tight right volte, while the right aids merely continue the previous activity more softly (shoulder-in), until in the next moment—drawing in, it presses the horse to the left, while these, just as before toward travers, counter-bend the right. There is then a breath of *renvers* present, which either immediately transitions to counter shoulder-in, the right aids swinging in continuous attachment into the tight left volte, whereupon the cycle is complete and begins anew; or the transition to renvers is executed with a bit more accentuation, after which the right aids behave imperceptibly, the left drive imperceptibly, and the change occurs.

More difficult—especially when the entire cycle is passed through in counter-canter—is to intentionally maintain the breath of *renvers* (thus travers in counter-canter) for several strides without inducing a change.

This rapid permeation of the horse through the rider's aids, completed in two, at most three strides, naturally already denotes a high level of dressage beyond practical necessity.

Yet for the lower levels, the same shaping of the horse occurs in the canter. Here the fact emerges, even visually, that the doctrine of crookedness brings about a transformation of the previous illusion.

A horse in left lead canter in counter shoulder-in position would nowadays find just as little approval among most riding instructors as its mirror image (horse right lead canter in counter shoulder-in position).

In the end, both are, for someone who begins canter work as early as possible, an entirely unavoidable consequence of the horse's crookedness.

By "as early as possible," however, I do not mean, as one so often sees today, cantering horses that are held in front and cannot yet carry themselves, and therefore lie on the hand. One must also not think of the images (charging, plunging, without posture rushing forward) which have hitherto been associated with horses placed outward.

Rather, by "as early as possible" I mean: beginning the canter without delay as soon as the horse can remain permeable in it, i.e., as soon as it carries itself on all four legs and thereby goes forward of its own accord—thus with a horse that moves in a broad frame yet fully fills it.

For the adherent of *Natural Horsemanship*—who neither actively constrains nor forces lateral positioning, but lets both develop of themselves—this occurs in the average horse within a few days. Naturally, however, only in the innate crooked position! This is now, on the left rein—taking the horse from Chapter V as an example—a kind of counter shoulder-in. The horse is "permeable" only in this form and in no other, neither in walk, nor trot, nor finally in canter, indeed not even in the jump (cf. here the highly interesting experiments of Mr. von Tepper-Laski[52] in "*Rennreiten*"[53] on the saddle-less jumping of crooked horses under riders who yield to their horse in the initial jumps).[54]

For one who knows crookedness and makes use of it, no other position at all comes into consideration for the left lead canter; and proof of the correctness of the position is obtained, as always, from the horse itself, which now enters the canter calmly and remains calmly within it. One can therefore also work in it without further ado.

Just as in the trot, and under exactly the same favorable conditions as there, we thus begin without delay the straightening formation, driving through gradual increase of right bend the horse more and more into the left rein, in order to gain with this all the more thoroughly and reliably the left poll bend—our final goal—as a matter of course.

Quite different is the situation with the right lead canter! It too is begun as early as possible, i.e., as soon as a tolerable permeability for the left aids is ensured. I note here that a moderate degree of permeability sufficient for the canter is reached quite soon, especially if one deliberately allows the nose to go somewhat outward. Further details consult Chapter VI; only full permeability and poll bend to the left require here, as everywhere, much time, effort, and patience. Earlier it is impossible!

A horse pressing outward cannot canter with swing nor in self-carriage; and before the aforementioned permeability is attained, the horse in question is in this form that allows no control. Yet even the achieved permeability is only a makeshift one. The horse will continue to succumb to its natural urge to fall outward with the left hind leg and must therefore be counteracted with equal persistence.[55]

Thus we require counter shoulder-in! But apart from that, it cannot be dispensed with. The value of straightening—by which we mean sharper, more direct, and more decisive effort than any previous method has practiced—we do not interrupt for a single moment! Now the horse has, in this work, reached precisely the point at which its reshaping has arrived at the stage where counter shoulder-in is the action that increasingly abolishes its crookedness.

Consequently—we must ride it as well! The horse does not place itself left of its own accord—in contrast to the right positioning in left lead canter; we initially permitted that, so to speak, under compulsion, in order not to disturb permeability and thereby to reach reshaping more easily with and within it—no, I place it left because its stepping forward into the right rein is insufficient for me.

---

[52] *von Tepper-Laski, A 19th-century German cavalry officer and riding theorist and authority on fast riding. - Translator's note.*

[53] *"Rennreiten" literally means riding at speed (from rennen = to run at full speed). In 19th–early 20th century German riding literature, especially military and technical texts, it refers to: a) riding at full gallop or near-maximum speed, b) the seat, balance, and aids required for fast riding, c) practical riding for cavalry, couriers, hunting, cross-country, and racing pace, d) emphasis on security, light seat, forward balance, not manege schooling. It is a functional category of riding, not a sport discipline.*

[54] *Most horses will simultaneously also "go down"; with difficult temperaments, however, "going forward" alone suffices entirely, provided only the first condition—self-carrying without hanging on the rein—is truly fulfilled. Giving down in such cases brings about no correction faster and more thoroughly than precisely the canter.*

[55] *The advantage of counter-positioning with an outward-pressing horse was, incidentally, already well known to the old Seidler [the old master]. What he recognized purely empirically appears here to us as a logical consequence of the doctrine of crookedness.*

And likewise the horse presses inward with the hindquarters; conversely it would much rather go straight ahead. I do not tolerate this, because I feel that the entire left side is not yet yielding, the right aids not yet sufficient to allow correct poll work with the latter. In short, I position the horse so because, for the time being, only in this position does the impulsion of the hindquarters fully—spring forward, allowing the back oscillations to remain in their flow, and I remain in this position as long as necessary. On the other hand, I also do not ride a second longer in this position than necessary. The more the horse swings forward to the right, the more these aids assert themselves, until a travers-like canter arises—and thus the work continues further, exactly as chapter five explains.

But I am already anticipating Chapter Seven too far.

Chapter Six
The Hard and the Soft Side of the Horse

The author's notes end with chapter five.—Neither the promised chapter on the aids for the bent or crooked horse, nor that on the hard and the soft side, has been written. I shall attempt, in both cases, to step in myself.

With the hard and the soft side it is, in fact, a curious matter.

In order to come immediately in medias res, I refer to the author's remarks on the resistance of the horse's hind legs whenever the transition from left shoulder-in to right travers begins. The prerequisite for the innate condition of the horse under discussion was consistently the following:

"The horse accepts the right rein; with the left hind leg it evades laterally."

Through right shoulder-in the horse had come onto the left rein, then through left travers had been deeply bent to the left, and thereafter led into "left shoulder-in." Now the left hind leg, after it had been made sufficiently yielding that, with support of the left rein, it willingly stepped toward the horse's centerline, was to receive the final polish by being compelled to step across also over the previously only loosely guided right hind leg, even when the latter itself was already well brought under and moving more slowly.

There can be no doubt that it—the left—was and is the sole bearer of the difficulty. But who now appears to resist? By no means the left, but rather the right hind leg!

The horse feels this quite precisely: if I step willingly forward with the right hind leg, the left must bend more a second later, and the pain, the discomfort, the compulsion—whatever one may call it—in the left hind leg asserts itself. The horse therefore resists more readily the aid that demands the stepping-under of the right hind leg; and among a thousand riders scarcely one will be clear that the cause here is to be sought solely in the left hind leg, and that the refusal of the right is mere deception.

Consequently, they will also scarcely proceed correctly, that is, return at the same moment to "left shoulder-in," there grasp the stirrup under higher guidance and sharper resistance, and then, upon returning to the old loading relationship, once again seek the right-travers bend. Another correct path—leaving energetic struggle aside—would also be to continue riding right travers, thus continuing to demand the bend as before, but by slightly deeper lowering of the forehand or by a somewhat wider frame of the whole horse, momentarily impose on the left hind leg only a slightly greater load when stepping over the still well-maintained right to demand less in that moment when resistance began, so as not to place the left colleague in embarrassment.

I cite both paths in order to characterize the continual interplay between balance—direct loading of the hind legs through higher carriage and engagement—and correct muscular development—obedient yielding before the aids that demand lateral suppleness—as the means with which we chiefly work in practice and achieve a training that is equally solid and rapid and effortless for both parties.

Against the direct, powerful, naturally yet at the same time moderate improvement of balance, no horse resists, so long as one avoids, by the well-known means—high, light, mobile hand with driving seat—bringing the muscles into congestion, which inevitably occurs as soon as we simultaneously demand direct lateral suppleness.

Likewise—self-evidently only with loosened muscles—the horse has nothing to object to a direct, powerful, naturally moderate demand for lateral suppleness, provided that one avoids, in doing so, bringing more weight onto the hindquarters than they have already become accustomed to carrying comfortably.

Now we know from chapter one that any overloading of the hindquarters beyond the measure that has already become second nature to them instills in the horse the urge to stretch forward–downward and in doing so to take as much elastic contact as possible and to lengthen itself as much as we desire or require. The more we initially allow this overloading before establishing balance, the broader the frame becomes, the more powerfully it springs elastically into the hand.

Do we not possess in these factors all the means for the quickest and yet effortless shaping of the horse for both parties? We improve the balance as much as the horse can bear it, maintain it there until we perceive that the limit of momentary carrying capacity approaches. Then we allow the eagerly desired weight-balancing to occur and use the resulting contact for shaping the musculature, which at the same time begins to lengthen, by means of lightly swinging movements of the hand—the seat swings in the same sense and kneads the back laterally through—thereby stimulating the horse to equal movement.

In this continuously sustained movement, the horse then shapes its spinal column and the muscles that move it by itself, without the slightest exertion arising for the rider. For just as, when improving balance, we evade any stiffening of the musculature by correct height and mobility of the hand, so here we avoid, as far as possible, any backward effect that loads the hindquarters.

We therefore fundamentally separate, at first, the improvement of balance and the shaping of musculature, in order at every point of engagement to achieve intensive effects with the lightest aids (small aids, great results—conservation of the rider!).

At the same time, the carrying capacity of the hindquarters rests during this shaping of the musculature, and the latter in turn finds recovery during the direct improvement of balance (alternation of effort whenever fatigue threatens!—conservation of the horse!).

Natural Horsemanship

Thus, through this eternally renewed alternation, we almost playfully extend the performance limits of both factors governing the horse, and with almost surprising speed reach the point where these limits at first touch, then increasingly flow into one another, become one.

Then the horse is simultaneously in balance and through—that is, collected.

Added to this is the fact that both factors complement one another reciprocally. The more the balance improves, the more easily the muscles form; the greater the suppleness, the more readily balance establishes itself.

Herein lies the astonishing power of this work; it is so great that a first-class[56] rider often brings a totally ruined horse into ordered form within minutes and fully corrects it in two to three weeks. This, however, is relatively incidental. For the troop, the value of a system is not measured by whether with it the first class achieves something—even the most outstanding—but rather by whether it teaches the average man to ride the horse in all gaits with sufficient balance and sufficient suppleness.

Our author required of every recruit, as the conclusion of arena work, two things: medium gallop in swinging, bounding strides at faultless distances and on the reins lying on the neck (high balance), and a calm raising of the forehand on the spot through seat and gentle spur, with the lightest possible hand (slowly swelling engagement of the muscles of the back).[57] I believe that the method which accomplishes this satisfies both the demands of the terrain and the necessity of employing the recruits in the second year in dressage work.

---

[56] *Works consciously or unconsciously by exploiting crookedness.*

[57] *From these two final requirements placed upon the recruit, which relate solely to the horse going straight ahead, it also follows that such active aids as swinging hands are not demanded for use by the troop, as footnote 29 on p. 42 already emphasized.*
For the "sufficient" suppleness of the troop, the doctrine of the natural crookedness already fully comes into its own, provided one is content never to force positions with the hand, but rather to wait for what, with light guidance, a well-driving seat in general—and in particular through increased use of the leg, passive holding of the rein against which the horse momentarily presses more strongly (cf. p. 76), as well as through frequent changes of contact—results of itself in lateral suppleness.
If, nevertheless, these aids are accorded thorough consideration here, this lies in the fact that a doctrine as new and untested as that of the natural crookedness is directed in the first instance to the advanced rider, who thinks independently and sets himself higher goals. What, however, can be made usable for the troop from this doctrine is an entirely different question. In this respect it is only to be pointed out here that the absolute correctness of a doctrine does not for that reason alone make it usable for the troop.
Here, too, the best is often precisely the enemy of the good! Rather, for a "riding instruction," the art consists precisely in finding, from among the many good things, that good which is usable for the troop. Only because this is not always understood does riding instruction appear to many clever people—who are nevertheless not familiar with the nature of the troop—as being "in need of improvement." In spite of everything, it is still today the best for the troop that we have and will be, should it appear necessary, timely—without the urging of the uncalled-for—be reshaped; not replaced (that is improbable, since its fundamental conceptions are unshakably correct), but reshaped.

The Hard and the Soft Side of the Horse

I ask forgiveness for this digression, which, however, as will be shown, also has relevance for the question of the hard and the soft side. I return to the latter by repeating that, at the moment when the horse refuses the right travers bend, the left hind leg is the actual bearer of the resistance, while the right appears to oppose.

Exactly the analogous phenomenon confronts us with regard to the hard and the soft side as such.

First it should be pointed out that the designations "hard" and "soft" prove themselves to be entirely unusable.

For the rider A, who straightens crookedness, thanks to the preserved swing of the back, the horse is never "hard;" instead, the horse comes more powerfully and elastically to one rein than to the other. With the holding rider B, if he is not a master of the art, the horse indeed becomes "hard" of necessity. (Proof of both may be found in the concluding word to chapter five.) In any case, what is common to both riders is the stronger contact on one hand. Let us therefore provisionally replace the expression "hard" with "stronger," and the expression "soft" with "weaker" contact.

Now then, A will call one and the same horse "more strongly connected" on the right, B on the left, according to current usage therefore "hard," and will call the respective opposite side "soft," and above all will also feel it so.

This fact appears highly strange at first glance, entirely clear at the second. A, accustomed to taking the horse as it is, not forcing it between the reins, but adapting his aids to the horse's capacity for feeling, will use the compliance of the convex right side for his influence, while initially sparing the sensitivity of the concave left. He feels that, without provoking resistance, he can act quite strongly on the right, but on the left only very gently; he therefore quite naturally calls the horse more strongly connected on the right, more weakly on the left.

B therefore immediately takes on a remount which, although somewhat crooked, is powerfully driving and holding, a horse that presses strongly into the bit; when bridled, the right (diagonal) side suffers relatively little pain here, since it can yield to the opposing aids—but the left! If the right hind leg is opened, then it is here, through the convexity of the neck, as it were closed off. For this very reason the horse does not of its own initiative come up to the left rein. If this is now forced upon him, then the muscles cannot suddenly assume the demanded form of suppleness; instead there arises merely a compression of the musculature. The horse will, quite apart from pain and conscious stiffening, with necessity become firm on the left and, for the average rider, also statically "hard."

One therefore cannot speak at all of "hard" and "soft," nor likewise of "stronger" and "weaker contact." Everyone understands something different by these terms, depending on how he is accustomed to handle the horse.

But also from another direction the expressions "stronger" and "weaker contact" fail to capture the essence of the matter.

The horse which the author presented to us in chapter five was worked straight exclusively by first obtaining a "stronger" contact on the left through improvement of the corrupted right shoulder-in (without a pushing left hind leg), then progressing to this lesson in improved execution (left hind leg fully springing into the rein). In the following left travers and left shoulder-in, the right rein again received the fuller feel, until finally in right travers this role again fell to the left.

I insert here that simultaneously unreserved and supple coming up to the left rein—this is the ultimate goal for the horse in question with regard to the rein. Right travers represents the highest task for the horse.

The sequence of tasks is as follows:

Right shoulder-in = swinging the left hind leg toward a non-demanding, rather willingly receiving hand and into the rein, with the horse's weight swinging into it.

Left travers [haunches in left] = the bringing-under is strengthened to such a degree that even counter-bending against the left rein is tolerated; but still with support from weight swinging from right to left.

Left shoulder-in = the bringing-under is strengthened to such a degree that counter-bending is tolerated even when the weight swings from left to right, that is, from the left rein.

Right travers [haunches in right] = the culmination! But bringing-under to the left rein with the greatest possible engagement, because here—apparently—counter-bending is absent; this is pure suppleness.

By nature, however, the horse was precisely because of the absence of coming-up, stiff on the left and unsupple, as immediately became apparent when yielding was demanded there (cf. Rider B); now the suppleness on the left is so high that it is fully present even in this position, because and insofar as the horse comes up on the left.

I believe this observation to be highly interesting.

Elastic bringing-under and suppleness are so intimately connected that at the highest level they coincide.

Thus the designation "stronger," "weaker" contact is also unusable. The sides of the horse alternate continuously in this respect.

We can therefore, without misunderstandings of every kind, in *Natural Horsemanship, 2nd edition*, analyze matters, and thus speak only of a difficult and a somewhat less difficult, or a favorable and an unfavorable, or a dominant and a submissive side; otherwise a theoretical understanding of crookedness and correct straightening is not possible. For practice this is, of course, irrelevant, since in working, as we have seen, the contact changes of itself along the path of muscular execution that carries this change.

To For the initial stage to be considered successfully completed, two things must be accomplished:
1. the rider has allowed the horse to find the correct initial side and has avoided confusing the two sides through a false beginning of the work.[58]
2. The horse then comes more readily to the other rein and is able to settle on both sides.

Once both of these are true, it is useful to distinguish between one side that yields with lighter bringing-under and the other side that yields only with stronger bringing-under of the respective hind leg.

How we instruct our riders in such a way that they practically make use of crookedness in dressage for the quickest improvement of the horse remains reserved for chapter seven.

Here only a few further points are indicated.

First, the enormous importance of feeling the crookedness—not only for fine dressage work carried out with minutes instead of hours, but precisely for practice! No jockey, no gentleman rider can dispense with it. Only with it does a rider keep himself supple; only with it does a horse gallop in a back-saving and strength-sparing manner.

But further! Almost every campaign horse I have ridden was crooked, even if only slightly, although I must add that out of passion I ride only difficult horses and, wisely, also train only such. But I have also never yet heard that anyone else has seen a completely straight horse. All these horses are, as the author rightly says, entirely usable as "back-movers," i.e., soft, supple, powerful, and yet strength-sparing to bones and joints, if the rider positions himself in accordance with the momentary state of their crookedness. In the opposite case the back-movement quickly disappears, and the advantages mentioned above are lost.

Likewise, difficult and half-trained horses without the adjustment to crookedness, which has become second nature, are neither comfortable nor safe to ride without further measures.

The back-movement is truly seriously disturbed, however—fortunately only—when one actively interferes through the musculature and does not feel the crookedness. On average it suffices, as soon as neck and poll are in a light position, to leave the horse in peace, even if the nose occasionally strays, and to ride outside as much as possible solely with seat and leg. In any case it is wise to respond to any pulling not with strong resistance, but through good sitting, with a mobile, elevated, and at all times easily yielding hand.

Herewith I come to yet another property of the crooked horse which is likewise very important for dressage. It also explains why a rider of such astonishingly fine feel is nevertheless never quite finished with crookedness. This makes itself noticeable, as already indicated, in its full extent only when one allows the swing from the hindquarters to pass fully into the hand, accepts the

---

[58] *He must, like Rider A of our example, learn to think, feel, and act.*

connection, thus works directly toward shaping the musculature. Therefore it is indispensable for a system that is built upon it from the outset.

The less we intervene with the hand, the more imperceptible it becomes, until finally, in a horse ridden purely on balance with a lightly yielding nose, it remains perceptible only to one who is accustomed to take it as the starting point of his entire work insofar as it concerns the attainment of suppleness. I have already emphasized several times that the horse ceases to swing when, in the transmission of the swing to the bit, it breaks at hardened muscular points. The light hand and the lightly elevated nose do not disturb the muscular movement,[59] allowing the pain arising from resistance to escape forward, so to speak, into the air. Therefore all riders to whom the utilization of crookedness is not readily familiar should forbid themselves from shaping before they have secured a strong reserve of balance.

The author, in treating crookedness in chapter five, did not draw the final consequence from this fact—well known also to him—that crookedness makes itself less disturbingly noticeable the more the horse is ridden on balance.

He treated the question merely as if one were preferably working toward correct muscular shaping. According to his otherwise entirely correct exposition for this case, the sequence of modifications of the four lateral movements would be indispensable for straightening and suppleness of the horse exactly in the order he indicated. One could not ride diagonally right before one had securely established diagonally left, right-shoulder-in–like and left-travers–like gaits.

This is not entirely the case even for work that intervenes with the hand, insofar as some horses, whose irregular muscular shaping has its seat primarily in the neck, very quickly go powerfully into the left leg and rein, but accept the counter-bending of left travers only with difficulty. With these horses one makes faster progress if one uses powerful driving into the left aids in order first, in diagonal right, to make the left hind leg thoroughly obedient. Its improved bending ability then brings about, upon renewed demand for left travers, much more rapidly the correct yielding also at the poll.

But we can do exactly the same already earlier, if the horse is not yet swinging powerfully enough into the left rein to shape the muscles directly on it. Here too, without counter-springing of the musculature, we can without difficulty in diagonal right, but with omission of bending, catch the left hind leg sustainably and thereby, in familiar weight-balancing, induce the horse to a rapid and powerful stretching downward, i.e., to a coming-up into the left rein.

If we then ride right shoulder-in again with counter-springing of hindquarters and forehand, the horse will be far more willing and ready than before to accept the left rein, because the simultaneous hind leg will now develop a demonstrably increased thrust.

---

[59] *The same naturally applies to the horse ridden long and low. If one lays the reins entirely on the neck so that the horse stretches fully, then even in a markedly crooked horse scarcely anything of the crookedness is perceptible.*

Thus we proceed here in an entirely analogous manner as described for the so-called straightness in chapter one then at the beginning of this chapter. We first drive the horse under us with relatively high and yielding hand and then graciously accept as contact what the horse itself offers, insofar as it seems expedient to us, in order to use it for shaping the musculature.

In general, the lateral-movement conclusion of chapter five must not be taken as an absolute recipe. It is indeed more than a mere schema, which only by means of one example was intended to present the author's train of thought to the reader. Rather, it also actually provides the chain of corrections and bending sequences most frequently encountered in practice, which—while sparing the horse's sensitivity—nonetheless enormously promote straightening and thereby full obedience, full swing, full suppleness.

The more difficult the horse and the less accomplished the rider, the more emphatically this path is to be recommended. It is the greatest, but the safest detour, by which one gradually but all the more reliably approaches the difficulties that the left leg and left rein find in the unfinished horse, and finally eliminates them.

From this it is at once clear that the greater the art in the saddle and the less difficult the horse, the more permissible deviations from this path become. The well-trained mountaineer also takes direct paths to the summit, where the less practiced would never arrive without the serpentines of the beaten main trail!

But—there is a great difference! Everyone believes he can ride and therefore choose the shortest path, even the quite deficient rider; among non-professional pedestrians the analogous pathological self-deception does not prevail!

In the final analysis it is a matter of the combination of rider talent and horse difficulty whether one may intervene directly or not. One may establish the rule: Does the rider get through with moderate aids—go on! Does he not get through—stop!—stop!

But note well: with moderate aids! Otherwise the artist easily experiences, in the realm of lateral suppleness, the same thing we warned against on p. 47 concerning sharply grasping work on the straight line:

"Certain rider influences allow such horses to do all sorts of things; if one leaves them to themselves, the lasting results are often alarmingly small."

Finally, one more point must be addressed: According to the idea most riders form—and to which the author himself, repeatedly in chapters two, three, and four, though only through carelessness of expression,[60] fell victim—the sharp raising of the nose is required for back-movement. Nothing is more false! This is the same fallacy, the same confusion of cause and effect, to which in general the work from front to back owes its temporary legitimacy.

---

[60] *From many other passages it emerges that the author correctly understands back-movement; compare above all the concluding remark to chapter two.*

Because the horse set into full balance lets the nose fall of itself, one mistakenly sought in the visibly elevated nose—regardless of where it came from and how much the balance suffered thereby—the criterion of essential progress.

And because the horse, in the final energetic release and now powerfully "swinging" back musculature, lightly leaning into the rider's hand, of itself sets the nose vertically—although this may still require encouragement despite everything—one just as falsely concludes: If I set the nose vertically, then I create back-movement, regardless of whether the muscles are freely swinging or are bracing themselves against the rider's hand.

The author seems (on p. 20-21) almost to have anticipated that the word "back-movement," despite all the distinctions with which von Holleuffer surrounded this concept in his very thorough explanation, would nevertheless be misunderstood—though not foreseeing how much and in which direction.

For back-movement in fact means nothing other than "back swinging" (the expression used by von Holleuffer, incidentally almost exclusively, though unfortunately also interchangeably with back-movement).

To interrupt the swing therefore means: to lose back-movement.

Nothing, however, breaks the swing more than resistance against unsolved musculature.

And conversely: Swinging movement means *eo ipso* [by the fact itself] back-movement—even if perhaps not yet fully perfected and refined fully mastered by the rider—regardless of whether the neck is carried high or low, the nose lightly advanced or sharply drawn in.

Nothing, however, promotes swing so much as driving into and under a light hand.

This clarification was indispensable in order from the outset to counter the objection that although there is constant talk of back-movement and its advantages, it would in fact be absent if the crooked horse were permitted initially to choose neck and head position freely at the rider's hand.

Chapter Seven
About the Rider's Aids on the "Bent" or Crooked Horse.

The preposition in the heading has not been inserted without intent. This chapter ought, properly speaking, to form a parallel to chapter three with regard to lateral aids, since in that chapter the doctrine of the aids for the direction from back to front was treated. But although we do indeed find all the effects discussed in chapter three again in a lateral direction, to classify them systematically and discuss them in sequence is both theoretically impossible and practically worthless. This is for the same reason: because there are even fewer "normal aids" in the lateral sense than there are for the direction from back to front.

Here, too, we find the explanation in the horse's innate crookedness.

First of all, as a result of its existence, we in a sense have two horses beneath us. Aids which one side willingly accepts are resisted by the opposite side; aids which have a dressage-promoting effect there are here directly harmful. Furthermore, the degree and the nature of the physical crookedness vary with every horse, and likewise in every stage of dressage of the same horse, and with these factors the distribution of the aids also changes accordingly.

Finally, the aids vary according to the moment of schooling in which rider and horse find themselves with regard to straightening, according to the horse's compliance or resistance to the aids, the line that is to be taken, etc., in such a kaleidoscopic manner that no question of systematic classification can arise.

Such a classification could only create confusion and is therefore practically worthless. All the more so since all these difficulties and subtleties, which awaken the feeling that a theory taking them into account might perhaps be of value to riding masters but never to the simple campaign rider of any sort, disappear at a stroke and are resolved by the harmlessly adopted seat of the simplest beginner, as soon as he has merely been brought to this seat and knows that he must never "deliberately" place his horse on the bit, but that this can only occur through the horse itself, and that this position will with certainty be a crooked one.

He must further, of course, know that this position is the one which is "initially straight for this horse," that is, that he must transmit every demand that comes to him in such a way to the horse that the self-chosen position, degree of flexion, etc., does not change beyond what results from the demand itself. A horse which of its own accord stands two inches to the right, for example, counts for him as sharply left-positioned, even though it still stands one inch to the right, and as very weakly right-positioned even though it stands a full two and a half inches to the right, etc.

If he observes this, then the crookedness is at first not present for him at all; it is eliminated. He can reinforce, half-halt, turn right and left, prepare the horse for the canter, etc., without disturbing the suppleness from back to front, insofar as the horse possesses it at all.

How he later improves the crookedness does not yet belong here. It was only a matter of showing two things:
1. that no artificially mysterious things are demanded of the young rider any more than before, and
2. that when we now release the beginner, not only does a balance from back to front exist, but also laterally, which is indispensable and must be taken into account in practice.

It is exactly, as explained in chapter three for the direction from back to front, the precondition for weight aids as for all other aids. With it, we have in the shortest time a freely let-go, aid-accessible horse, without ever coercing him.

The short practical conclusion from this reads as follows: There is no inner and outer side with respect to the hand, the circle, the volte, or whatever line we may be riding; the position of the horse as well as the rider's seat depends rather exclusively on the combination of the bend corresponding to the line being ridden and the innate crookedness. And furthermore: it is an error to believe that a horse must be positioned to the right for right canter and to the left for left canter. This is of course the final goal, but in the work only the feeling that develops of itself through surrender to the horse's movement can find the momentarily correct—suppleness-producing—position and the seat adapted to it, which then gradually corrects itself toward one corresponding to the bend of the canter.

That many riders notice little or nothing of this on average horses, in my view, proves nothing about the rider, only about the slight difficulties of these horses. The characteristic itself exists in every horse. What we today call a particularly difficult horse is almost always a pronouncedly crooked horse. These are the true teachers for the more advanced rider.

I still vividly recall one of the best horses I have ever mounted. It was a gelding of striking size, with the shortest and most energetic back in the world, a long, noble neck, iron legs—in short, an ideal, and at first glance without any difficulty other than his enormous power.

The owner was regarded in the regiment as an excellent rider, but after scarcely fourteen days with this horse was so finished that in the true sense of the word he could no longer ride a single step with him. Mounting was immediately followed by bucking, canter attacks, head-throwing, bolting and stiffening; in short, the matter was over. Finally, I was asked to mount the horse. From merely looking at him it was already clear to me that the crookedness was the principal cause of the unrest. In fact, after about ten minutes we were completely in agreement—but only in a left counter-shoulder-in of such strength that the hindquarters were placed a full step away from the forehand, the nose standing at least half a foot to the right. On the right rein the horse was completely soft; on the left he came to the hand with about fifty pounds of pressure, but entirely elastically. Three days later the displacement of the hindquarters necessary for suppleness was reduced to about half a foot; in front the yielding of the left travers bend had already begun. The pressure on the left rein when riding through to travers amounted to only about ten pounds; walking on long reins was possible; in short, everything toward straightening had been initiated, and the improvement progressed rapidly from day to day.

In left canter, however, I still had to ride for weeks with strong right positioning, a seat strongly urging the right hind leg inward, if I wished to be certain of suppleness.

Likewise, I still presently own a Thoroughbred mare who had previously always returned to the dealer's stable because she bolted without restraint. With her as well, the solution of the riddle lay solely in the high degree of crookedness. She is now so supple that with careful shaping through the aforementioned sequence of lateral movements, the mane crest flaps from one side to the other in exact correspondence with the respective bend—a result which, given her original stiffness, I believe was quite remarkable and is in our modern riding not at all common. Nevertheless, she still goes strong right canter even today most elastically only in pronounced left positioning. She can, of course, also be positioned to the right here, but the passage of the swing to the forehand still takes place more playfully, more comfortably, and thus more springily when her innate crookedness is taken into account. *Naturam ne furca quidem expellas!* ["You cannot drive out nature, not even with a pitchfork."!]

I ask that the presentation of personal experiences not be taken amiss. Since I write anonymously, this alone proves that the sole intention is to advance the matter.

Here in particular, I believe that by presenting these two horses I have very clearly illustrated the first conclusion—that the bend into which one must take the horse is almost entirely independent of the rein on which one is riding—and at the same time provided the transition to the closely connected second conclusion:

Which aids must predominantly take effect in a turn, on the circle, in lateral movements, in the canter, etc., is likewise relatively independent of the line being ridden.

One therefore cannot, when giving the aids for a particular lesson, say, for example: "the inner rein must be used to bend, the outer to straighten; the inner leg must drive laterally, the outer restrain; the rider must sit somewhat toward the inner side," etc. For a fully trained horse these aids may be quite appropriate; in dressage work with an unfinished horse, however, there is not much to be accomplished with them. Rather, here too the resistance against the aids of one side and the yielding obedience to the aids of the other side play the far more decisive role.

Let me take, for example, the horse first mentioned, which can be briefly characterized as follows: crooked in exactly the same sense as that assumed in chapters five and six. It of its own accord accepts the right leg and rein, allows itself to be influenced by them; with the application of the left aids it becomes—incidentally, not from disobedience but from pain—excited.

At the beginning of the work, this horse had to be "taken up" with aids specifically suited to him. Allowing him to go forward in the normal manner was not possible, because he would simply run away. His natural crookedness had become so pronounced that, although the rider consciously yielded the sensitive left side, the hindquarters and forehand no longer worked in harmony and instead pressed against one another. The right hind leg stepped ever more strongly underneath the body and, in doing so, held the forehand fixed on the rein.

As soon as this occurs—marked by calmer, more controlled, slower stepping—I am ready for any demand, turning, circle—volte and canter would perhaps still be somewhat too much for such a sensitive horse—in the most fluid execution and without the slightest resistance on the part of the horse. Naturally, however, not with the previously used normal aids, but rather using those which have so far proven themselves to me as the aids that dominate the horse: the right ones. With them I press the horse from right to left, from the rail over onto the circle, thus actively turning only with the outer aids; the inner ones do indeed drive forward—but the forward-driving with the whole seat may never be lacking in any lesson, whatever it may be called—laterally, however, they have at most a receiving or preserving role.

The entire difference between this horse and the average horse (the same kind of crookedness being naturally assumed) lies solely in the degree of their crookedness. For the former, out of pain, the straight course of the back in any form other than the one described is directly impossible; it resists or becomes agitated and finally desperate. In the latter, such striking consequences do not occur, but even in him the full counter-springing of the musculature, the swinging of the back, suffers. That horse gains this—and with it calm—only when the hindquarters are displaced by a full step; this one perhaps needs scarcely a hoof-width. For both, however, it remains indispensable:
1. to find this position, and
2. to take it into account with every demand (turning, etc.).

The same applies later, when the progressive straightening of the horse, as the author sets forth in chapter five, b-rings it into another position relative to the track: depending on the momentary condition, the lateral aids must therefore be contra-shoulder-in-like, travers-like, shoulder-in-like, or *renvers*-like. Otherwise we interrupt the swing, i.e., damage the horse and make our work more difficult.

The thus markedly crooked gelding finally leads me over to the third contradiction of the aids of today's prevailing theory. I mean the principle that the outer aids should not be used until the inner ones have gone through.

About the Rider's Aids on the "Bent" or Crooked Horse

Correctly understood, of course, this principle is entirely ours—but

1. it does not refer to the right or left side of the horse, but solely one-sidedly to crookedness. On this point I can spare myself further elaboration; reference to the manner in which the gelding should be transferred onto the circle suffices. Fundamentally, this contradiction with today's theory is only another manifestation of the already discussed point: that there is no right-hand and left-hand turning on the track which would require a change of bend. No matter how often the hand changes, the bend always remains the same.[61]

But we also understand,

2. by the demand to use the outer aids only when the horse yields to the inner ones, never and under no circumstances that they are ever completely removed from the horse.

I ask here as well to be allowed to revert to the gelding. A sharp critic must immediately have noticed that the manner in which this horse was supposed to go after ten minutes stood in contradiction to the views represented.

Contrary to the assertion of chapter five, that one can initially work only on the favorable side because only there does the horse carry more readily, but not on the difficult side, the gelding should after ten minutes be entirely soft on the favorable side, but on the difficult side take the rein with about fifty pounds of elastic pressure.

That, however, is precisely—to put it trivially—the core of the entire doctrine of crookedness: if I immediately place the horse straight ahead, it becomes "hard" on the difficult side, and this fault of "hardness" clings permanently to all further work as a hindrance to any progress. The more one then works on the hard side, the harder the horse usually becomes.

If, on the other hand, I place the horse, according to its innate muscular formation, from the outset crooked and demand suppleness with the favorable side, then the horse goes to the difficult side as well—and indeed immediately, elastically, and willingly.

Immediately, elastically, and willingly!—Because with the strengthening of the concave bend on the right there is also connected a strengthening of the convex bend on the left. Immediately: the threshold at which pain would arise through compression of the convex muscles is pushed far outward. Elastically: because the hardened muscle bundles are stretched and thereby loosened. Willingly: because the connection mouth–hand becomes longer on the horse's side, not on the rider's—provided only, and here we return to the question of the outer aids, that the outer hand does not evade, but remains soft and yet receptive at the horse's mouth.

---

[61] *Of course, we are always speaking here of the unfinished horse, not yet "hollow" and bent on both sides. Once dressage has achieved this, the bend naturally changes with the hand.*

Natural Horsemanship

We must even go one step further! Even according to our explanations it still seems as though bending to the right were the main thing, the stretching of the left muscles merely a pleasant but still only a secondary effect.

Only now do we reach the core of the matter!

The situation is exactly the reverse! The sole purpose of right bending is the stretching and lengthening of the left neck muscles grown rigid by nature, in order to loosen and make them supple. Only when this has first been achieved can it succeed in bending them hollow and thereby also bringing the naturally concave right side, which has too little muscular tension, into elastic tension.

In a word: for natural schooling there is no right and left side at all, but only a crooked neck as such. Both sides are out of order; therefore the aids of both sides must be continuously active.

And with that we come to the practical execution of shaping the neck.

We simply set it into a swinging lateral movement, but from the very first moment not with one hand, but with both hands shaping the entire neck; not evenly to both sides, but initially increased toward the side to which the horse yields most willingly; not with equal, but with differently strong swinging hands.

Through this differentiation in the work we take crookedness into account—but now no longer on the basis of theoretical consideration or long-winded instruction to the rider. No, we simply let the horse itself tell us, according to its crookedness, by giving it the following simple principle for treating the unresolved musculature:

"Swing with each hand as strongly as the horse already tolerates, but as lightly as the horse still tolerates."

In doing so we think solely of the resistance that the horse sets against our swinging hands, and do not concern ourselves at all with the resulting position. That shows itself to us from the horse itself, and we receive the following initial picture:

Right (favorable side)—more powerful swing of the hand;

Left—the hand merely accompanying the mouth by suction and at the same time keeping the base of the neck straight[62] through correct lateral position; far to the right swinging nose, then the nose snapping back into the old position.

This picture, however, remains the same only for a short time. It gradually and without perceptible transition shifts more and more in the sense that the more swing flows into the left hand during the right-swinging, the more it also participates in the backward swing to the left, and correspondingly the right hand applies ever less force for the right swing, the more the horse follows the increasingly lighter, finally merely indicative aids of this hand through unceasing repetition.

---

[62] *Cf. note on page 106.*

About the Rider's Aids on the "Bent" or Crooked Horse

Thus the principle according to which we measure the strength of our swings for unresolved musculature gradually passes over into the other one governing resolved, or resolving, musculature: "As light as possible, but as strong as necessary," whereby it again concerns itself solely with the overcoming of resistance encountered by the swinging hands.

The final picture would ultimately be:

On the right only an indicative, on the left a powerful swing; to the right only moderately, then over straight ahead swinging to the left nose.

This leads us over to achieving hollow bending of the left side (travers-like).

Between the initial and final picture there naturally lies yet a moment in which the resistance of the neck muscles to the hands has become approximately equal. As soon as this is the case, the right hand again begins to demand the bend more vigorously and let's go more briskly as soon as the self-active snap back to the left occurs. The left hand, on the other hand, goes along fully when the right hand demands, in order not to hinder the swing, but then also supports the snapping back through more vigorous demand on its part. In doing so it directs the rein sharply toward the place on the neck (two to three hands' breadth behind the poll) where the muscles, still in an unresolved state, press outward (bulge), and the nose springs beyond the innate position to the left.

With continued repetition there soon comes the moment when at first individual strands of the mane swing over to the left now here, now there, and now it is time, swinging ever more actively, almost without regard, to stimulate the muscles. Above all, one must swing more powerfully to the right: the greater the action in that direction, the greater also the reaction, the self-activity of the horse. The more it succeeds at the same time in executing the swings purely laterally, without backward effect on the hindquarters[63] and without compressing the freely floating neck, the sooner that long-desired moment occurs when the entire mane swings from right to left, and thereby also outwardly indicates that the neck is now truly bending hollow along its entire length.

Meanwhile, in this process the left hand will be the one that encounters increased resistance, because the new bend is still unfamiliar to the horse, while the old one is constantly sought again. If, however, we continue the swinging always in accordance with the principle *"As light as possible, but as strong as necessary,"* now also with the aim of progressively strengthening the left bend, while allowing the nose to swing over to the right only indicatively, then the horse yields ever more willingly to the left hand with each leftward swing of the nose, which therefore can act ever more lightly and must. At the same time,

---

[63] *The swings are nevertheless possibly very powerful, especially on the rein where the increased resistance shows itself. Grown muscles cannot be shaped with merely playing aids. Yet they do not act back on the hindquarters if they correspond exactly to the muscular resistance without delay. They consume themselves in overcoming it, as can be observed in every truly "hard" horse. The fault there is precisely that, as a consequence of muscular resistance, the aids do not penetrate through to the hindquarters.*

however, it presses each time into the right rein, now located on the convex side, so that resistance there increases.

Finally there again occurs a moment in which the resistance in both hands is approximately equal and beyond that becomes greater on the right with each leftward swing of the left hand, as the right muscles enter ever more convex bend.

Then the main work is done! Once the hardened convex bend has been transformed into a concave one, the right rein full, the left loose, everything else is child's play![64]

The moment at which this tends to occur is, of course, a very variable one. It comes all the sooner the more the horse carries itself, the more the neck is a freely oscillating appendage, and the more the rider acts only by indication with the hands, allowing the horse to carry out the oscillations independently.

If the left hand, when the horse is turning to the right, receives against it, a pressure naturally arises there, and indeed one that is all the greater the more neglected the neck muscles are, the more sharply the neck as a whole is assembled, and the greater the horse's preponderance toward the forehand still is. In the much-cited Senner, this pressure was therefore also a considerable one, because this horse was exceptionally taken up immediately, before it carried itself; but even then the pressure remains—when the crookedness has been correctly taken into account—strong, yet elastic, similar to that of a rubber band under strong tension. This work nevertheless remains to be discouraged: even the horse correctly used in its crookedness works itself most effortlessly and most effectively when, at the same time, it goes in balance.

And with this we also come, for lateral work, from the entire neck to the entire horse.

Here too, as on the straight line, the hand alone contributes nothing, the effect of the driving aids, especially the seat aids, becomes evident! If we substitute, for the laterally oscillating activity of the hands, the same activity of the seat aids in timing, strength, and release—where the aids given on one side are released by those of the other side, with a light hand that merely accepts the result—their effect will become clear to us.

The relationship of their effect to that of the hands may perhaps best be compared to the horse's spine as a riding whip. The slightest lateral movement of the firmly connected rear end held in the hand causes the strongest snapping and swishing of the tip. Even if the neck is not as loose and flexible as the forward end of the whip, the matter is analogous for it nevertheless! If the rider succeeds in making the back swing laterally even slightly, the neck swings of its own accord and generously in response to merely breath-like indications of the

---

[64] *I would like to emphasize once again that the transformation has truly taken place only when the mane crest swings over to the formerly convex side and remains there. Otherwise the horse deceives the rider, sets the nose to the left, but nevertheless leaves the muscles more or less in convex assembly.*

hands—provided, of course, that it is not rigid—then the whip does not swing either—whereas even strong bending of the neck without driving and laterally swinging seat aids have no influence on the back.

How then do the lateral seat aids arise? Purely practically I have found—from the gait itself. As soon as the rider, on the one hand, drives well forward, and on the other hand, fully released, strives to remain in connection with the horse, to adapt his weight—so to speak breathing—to the constantly alternating weight shifts of the horse on both sides.

By the word "breathing" I mean that just as naturally and unconsciously as the chest breathes in and out, so it should become natural for the rider, step by step, to feel the autonomous swinging over and back of his weight through the horse's gait and to give himself up to it.

If the horse goes according to the rider's wishes, the rider thus gives no aids; this "breathing seat" is the seat of balance for the respective gait. Aids arise when the rider intentionally accelerates or retards this breathing movement toward one direction (right or left), as soon as he feels that the horse threatens to resist or hurry toward the opposite side.

Much more than this cannot be said without schematically breaking the total effect down into individual effects. Only one thing must not exist directly: error. Modern theory—I need only recall the well-known dispute as to whether, in shoulder-in, the rider should weight the inside or the outside—still lacks the concept of the bilaterally swinging seat altogether. According to it, the seat appears either hanging or standing on one side, whereas in truth the rider, sitting on both halves of the horse, in constant alternation depending on the moment of movement, weights now a bit outside, now inside, pushing (corresponding to the effect of the seat on the straight line) or accompanying (corresponding to the effect of weight).

In the concluding remarks to chapter five, I attempted to sketch the aids for the lateral gait cycle in the canter, but I do not in any way claim that these are incontrovertibly correct. Theory must not wish to penetrate more deeply here either than it is capable of doing. And all aids stand—especially the finer the matter becomes—in such intimate interrelation that the share of the individual ones can no longer be distinguished with full certainty.

For practice, however, I would like to recommend a method based on my experience that is extremely simple and fully proven, to make the lateral seat aids perceptible to the rider: namely, the breaking down of the aid required for a particular movement into several sub-aids that have already become familiar to the rider.

I choose as an example the most important lessons for the transformation of the crooked horse: counter-shoulder-in, travers, shoulder-in–like movement. Travers and *renvers* are relatively similar; shoulder-in, however, differs from counter-shoulder-in in that the former is initiated through a forehand turn, the latter through a hindquarters turn.[65]

I. Counter-Shoulder-In:
1. Halt! Seat action brings the entire horse into and under the hand; weight then remains.
2. Forehand right![66] Seat action presses the hindquarters from right to left (best achieved by a somewhat lively "rump turns right"), weight swings over onto the left hind leg.
3. Driving forward into the left rein (in natural flexion, i.e., as if one wanted to ride diagonally through the wall). Weight swings back again onto the inner (right) hind leg, in order to convert the sideways movement into forward movement; the seat at the same time strives powerfully forward through the wall.

Purpose: The right hind leg transfers the weight to the left one—which does not wish to step under—during "forehand right," and then an attempt is made, through riding forward, to keep this weight on the left for a moment.

II. Travers
1. Halt!
2. Forehand right!
3. Left volte!

— Halt! Forehand right! Exactly as in I. [above], only the aid for "forehand right" is much lighter, since the right hind leg has already learned to yield to a light indication.

Left volte—march! Weight swings so forcefully back to the right that not only riding forward into the left rein but also yielding on it is sought.

Purpose: Continued attempt to make the left hind leg—now already accustomed (through sufficiently long practice of counter-shoulder-in) to taking up rider weight—carry more through pressing toward the center of the body.

I note here that each of these aids represents a true cycle, i.e., the sub-aids interlock in such a way that each automatically calls forth the other again, above all the last calling forth the first, if the intended movement (counter-shoulder-in, etc.) is to be maintained.

If, for example, after "driving forward into the left rein" or after "left volte—march!" the rider does not give "halt!" in time, the horse leaves the intended track. As soon as one aid takes effect, the other must set in. "Forehand right" occurs with each stepping of the right hind leg; riding forward into the left rein or "left volte—march!" with each stepping of the left hind leg.

---

[65] *Naturally counter-shoulder-in can later be ridden exactly like shoulder-in, shoulder-in in the beginning like counter-shoulder-in; this depends solely on the horse's level.*
[66] *"Forehand right" is, of course, resolved by the third sub-aid so that only the intended positioning remains.*

About the Rider's Aids on the "Bent" or Crooked Horse

For III. Shoulder-In (here left), I have found the breakdown into:

"Across the whole arena—change! Halt! Press right with all aids!" (especially both reins) to be very reliable.

Here too, however, the constant repetition of the first aid after pressing right is the main thing; it occurs on the stepping of the right (outer) hind leg, pressing right after the stepping of the left hind leg. I prefer "across the whole arena—change!" to the volte, because riders here keep the outer hind leg better under them and pull less on the left rein.[67]

The seat proceeds here as follows: driving forward while maintaining good control of the outer hind leg (seat effect) and swinging the weight inward (weight effect), which lands on it when the inner hind leg steps, only to be transferred again to the outer hind leg during the "pressing right."

For practice, for the training of both horse and rider, the demanded continual renewal of the aids is the most important point. Rider and horse are uninterruptedly compelled to give shaping aids, to obey shaping aids. The training of both takes place in this system in exactly the same way; it coincides absolutely.

I would also like to remark that the manner in which one gives the seat aids can be very variable. One can achieve the weight shift just as well by twisting the rump as by a slight yielding in the hips sideways, thereby also bending the corresponding hip outward—stretching the upper body more or less, treading the stirrup more perceptibly or more loosely. All of this undoubtedly represents nuances of effect; but whoever does not learn this from the horse itself may perhaps learn mechanical movements from a book, but never life and impulse-arousing aids. I deliberately do not go into such uncontrollable subtleties that evade discussion based on reasons. The relaxed rider arrives at them practically quite on his own.

It must, however, be emphasized that there is absolutely no question of an unquiet seat, a rolling in the saddle, etc., as frighteningly depicted in some books of older theory that advocate immobility of the middle position. If the horse yields, then no rider is softer, more pliant, and calmer than the rider who is continually shaping with the seat; if it does not yield, then one does not resort to coarse seat aids, but to the well-measured spur, whose main purpose is to secure obedience precisely against the seat aids.

Above all, the rider learns to correctly measure the strength of the alternating aids and to adapt them to the sensitivity of the horse.

As already follows from the indication of the purpose of the spur, it is here, even more than on the straight line, nothing other than the continuation of the seat aids. If the seat strives forward, the leg also drives forward; if the former strives right or left, the latter also acts in the same sense. I do, however, mention here a method by which the recruit most easily learns this seat-inspired manner of leg action. About the activity of the leg itself, I remain silent.

---

[67] *For "across the whole arena—change!" the aids "pelvis turns left, right leg and rein steer sideways" have already previously become familiar to the rider.*

Only few teachers realize how little supple riders are in pelvis, hips, and thighs, i.e., in the connecting joints, how stiff and clumsy the muscles are there. Consequently, the seat aids themselves are already lacking, and with them, naturally, also the inspiration for the leg aids.

Now, just as with the horse we supple the muscles through movement, we proceed in the same way here. We practice simply the alternating and at the same time mutually interpenetrating dropping of the thighs, which we will later use in the dressage, but in such a way that the upper thigh and the seat must participate in it. Alternately, at first while halted and then also at the walk, we let the thighs drop so far that the corresponding seat bone actually disengages, then falls back again, at short intervals first followed by the knee and then by the lower thigh.

This is practiced for so long and so often until the movement, both with a swinging upper body and without any participation of it, shows complete freedom from constraint and the regularity of a clock pendulum. If one then gradually allows the movement to diminish to the mere dropping of the lower thighs, the now loosened musculature of the upper thighs and the hips will constantly allow both the former as well as the seat to swing along with it, especially if at the beginning one expressly demands a slight co-swinging in the hips.

Here too it becomes evident once again that precisely the most important and simplest things are those that tend to be neglected. For it is obvious that a man who has not even learned, at the halt, to execute the purely mechanical movement playfully and elastically will be unable, in trot and canter, to give elastic seat, upper-thigh, and lower-thigh aids. And it is equally clear that a man who from the very first day practices that mechanical movement in such a way that he ultimately carries it out instinctively and unconsciously will also retain it easily in trot and canter.

As long as the movement is practiced purely mechanically, it must always be carried out with reins on the neck. The horses then immediately know that the matter does not concern them, and there is no question of a dulling against the aids, as some gentlemen believe; as soon as they come together on the reins, full attention to the aids is present.

Moreover, the swinging of the horse's spinal column both forward and sideways is more extensive without reins and therefore much easier for the recruit to feel and to take up with his own body; and finally the man gains that indispensable independence of the seat from the hand. Talented recruits acquire, in eight to ten days, an impeccable seat that follows the movements of the horse.

In conclusion I would still like to address the degree of positioning toward the reins at the very beginning of the work, especially since misunderstandings could arise here through the frequent mention of Senners.

He was admittedly set far away from the reins, and the nose was also taken far around. But he was, first of all, an entirely exceptionally crooked horse, and secondly he was mounted directly, without being loosened through long, forward riding. With such horses and such a method, the degree of positioning results by itself. One gradually increases the bend until one feels that the outer neck muscles stretch sufficiently against the rein that holds the neck absolutely

About the Rider's Aids on the "Bent" or Crooked Horse

straight[69] at its base, in order to establish elasticity. The degree of positioning can therefore become very large.

For ordinarily this is by no means the case.

Above all, I ask that it be noted that, as explained in the introduction to chapter five, even the slightest deviations from the reins (e.g. the movements previously called bending, breaking-off, etc.) were counted by the author among the lateral movements. Therefore it is always only a matter of contra-shoulder-in-type movement.

Contra-shoulder-in, for example, is accordingly present everywhere where I press the horse with the inner aids (related to the bend) against the outer ones, in order to make these effective and without counter-bending. If, for example, on the left rein I ride a horse in a very wide frame, for which the eye goes straight ahead, and I merely press the neck into the left, passively receiving rein with the right rein,[70] then this too is a contra-shoulder-in-type movement.

As already mentioned, however, crookedness comes less and less to expression the more the horse opens up. Quite naturally! Since all muscles are lengthened, they are also less resistant than when collected. This is therefore also the given starting point for a normal shaping of the horse, i.e. one proceeding from the easiest, then gradually increasing—especially for the military horse with its relatively inexperienced rider.

It is only a matter of achieving the wide frame in such a way that the aids pass into and through the horse, in a word: that the horse fills out the frame, despite its width, through the thrust of the hindquarters.

And thus the circle of our considerations closes again, bringing us back to the starting point, to chapter one!

If, on the basis of the teachings developed there concerning balance, we succeed through good driving in bringing the over-burdening of the hindquarters under and into our light hand, then the horse vaults directly forward-and-downward. We need only inch by inch to lengthen the reins and, with well-maintained balance, to continue driving forward uninterruptedly, and the wide frame—yet nonetheless fully filled through the horse's urge forward-and-downward—is there.

Now we alternately shape the musculature that springs fully into it and elastically challenges the hand, and then, guiding again higher and lighter, improve the balance in constant circulation without muscular strain, as we already explained in Chapter 6.

Then both grow rapidly and reliably upon the firm foundation of *Natural Horsemanship*.

---

[69] *Without this, the muscles of the crest—on whose stretching everything depends—would be unable to remain supple. In truth, it is of course not the hand, but the well-applied outer seat and thigh aid that prevents the tipping-over at the withers. In the hand, even here, the effect is only indirect.*

[70] *Hidden from the spectator, the seat aids naturally also act here: on the right, pressing away; on the left, strongly driving forward. The outer aid merely lifts the former, preventing it from expressing itself outward.*

Chapter Eight
Plinzner System—Fillis—*Natural Horsemanship*

Chapter seven was originally intended to remain the last. However, insofar as the so-called *Natural Horsemanship* contains a polemic, it is entirely unavoidable to take a position with regard to the systems that stand today in the foreground.

Moreover, it must appear desirable to prove that *Natural Horsemanship* arose entirely independently of the doctrines of the newer systems.

Both aims are achieved by reprinting several articles which were published on this side even before the appearance of the one as well as the other system, and which unmistakably characterize our own position on the questions raised there.

The Plinzner system was first inaugurated by an article by its author in No. 65 of the "Militär-Wochenblatt" of 1886. [For the complete Plinzner article, see Appendix A, which the translator strongly recommends reading before proceeding with this chapter.]

This article contained only general principles, which appeared so outstandingly correct that a supportive endorsement of them seemed appropriate, in order to keep alive interest in the still unknown work that was to be expected.

Thus arose the following article in No. 85 of the "Militär-Wochenblatt" of 1886:

Are the Content and the Form of Today's Horsemanship in Harmony?[71]

> The essay in No. 65 of the "Militär-Wochenblatt" of 7 August 1886 strikes perfectly the quintessence of our present riding, as it is in fact personally executed by good riders.
>
> Our army possesses many such riders. All the more striking is it that nevertheless, as the author rightly says, this manner of riding has not made its way universally. One might think that these riders, in their instructional activity, would pass on to their pupils what they themselves have felt and experienced, and thus gradually make it common property. The author does

---

[71] The present article was published without author attribution in the "*Nichtamtlicher Theil*" (Unofficial Section) of the "*Militär-Wochenblatt*" No. 85 (16 October 1886). Such anonymity was standard practice in the journal for editorial essays and discussion pieces of a doctrinal or reflective nature. In the 1880s, the "*Militär-Wochenblatt*" frequently presented contributions on riding, tactics, and military theory as institutional commentary rather than personal opinion, even when written by identifiable officers or editors. The absence of a byline should therefore not be read as accidental, but as consistent with contemporary editorial convention. - Translator's note.

not pursue this point further; evidently, however, it has a significant share in the solution of the questions raised in his essay. I would seek the explanation for this peculiar phenomenon in the frequently made observation that precisely those good riders, as teachers, do not have their pupils ride as they themselves ride, do not have their horses work in dressage divisions as they themselves do.

The difference is as follows. When we see the good rider ride, he always works the entire horse; when we hear him as a teacher, he works almost exclusively the neck.

How is this to be explained? When the good rider rides himself, he works—so long as the horse does not evade him—uninterruptedly with driving aids (seat), and therefore all deviations from the normal, even when they actually arise from deficient footfall or deficient activity of the back, appear externally at the neck (through escaping from the contact, boring into the hand, throwing the head, etc.).

Thus the resistance at the neck is for the good rider the resultant of all resistances in the whole horse that oppose the regulated gait. While he seems to eliminate the former, he in truth has eliminated the latter. He brings the entire spinal column into regulated form, and as proof of this, the most mobile part of it, which for the eye deviates most easily and visibly, neck and head, remains in regulated form.

The good rider therefore cannot be blamed if he says to himself: *"So long as neck and head do not willingly remain in the appropriate position in the various sections, the matter is not yet in order! But if I have achieved this, then my horse is finished!"* In a word, he may see in the neck-and-head position the criterion for the total training of his horse.

But only for his own person! As a teacher he transfers his private experience in this form to other riders, and then has them always ride differently, work differently, than he himself rides or works.

And why is this? Because the fundamental error of our present average rider lies in the lack of driving aids! With the presence of these, however, stands and falls the right to regard neck-and-head position as the criterion of a horse's total training. For if the rider lacks the necessary energy of his driving aids, then the logically self-evident proposition: *"If the whole (the entire spinal column) has the correct form, then the part (neck and head) must also have it,"* is reversed into the logical consequence: *"Because the part has the correct (here naturally only apparent!) form, the whole must also have it."*

The temptation to this fallacy is admittedly great enough. A difficulty in recognizing the error already lies in the character of the driving aids themselves. They lie primarily in the seat, in the correct bearing of the rider's weight, and are therefore unconscious, instinctive. The good rider sits calmly for his own sensation, almost inactive on the horse, and therefore is not fully conscious of the power which he exerts through this apparently quiet, in truth extremely effective seat; thus he cannot make it clear to his pupils, cannot transmit it to them.

Moreover, precisely good riders tend not to value theory highly; in full awareness of their own ability they remain distant from book-learning. And yet it is precisely more recent writings—I name "v. Holleuffer, *Pillarenarbeit*," "Graf v. Geldern, *Das Gewicht in der Campagnereiterei*" (E. S. Mittler & Sohn, Berlin), "*Dressur junger Pferde auf Trense von einem alten Reiter*" (Theodor Ray, Kassel)—which clearly uncover the source of error, the confusion of cause and effect. Such books are especially suited to this task because they almost exclusively establish general points of view for dressage as a whole, motives for the principles of dressage, without going deeply into details. By this they avoid a great danger, which books formulated in detailed fashion, as well as the riding instructor who teaches according to them, can hardly escape. This danger lies in the technical terminology of riding, which does not coincide with the essence of the lessons it designates.

For it is unquestionably not logically correct, when the soft connection to the hand with deep nose is actually achieved by the rider's calm balance allowing the horse to find its balance as well, then to say: *"The horse is now on the bit."* It is not correct, when through driving the hindquarters and arching the back the whole horse is pushed together and with this the nose also comes more sharply forward, to speak of "contact." It is not correct, when the gait becomes more swinging on the straight line after alternating driving of the hind legs, to credit this success to the lesson "turning"!

This may seem petty, perhaps far-fetched! But one should consider that precisely these three lessons actually contain the entire riding education. A horse which
1. has let go and found its balance,
2. allows itself to be pushed together under arching of the back and swinging stepping-under of the hind legs, and
3. finally,[72] in light shoulder-in position, willingly places the inner hind leg alternately under the body, is as good as finished; a rider who correctly teaches these three lessons to a raw horse can do everything that is necessary for a campaign rider as a trainer. If he continues with the effects applied here, he will have the horse allow itself to be pushed together more and more from behind to front and sideways right and left from day to day, and thereby become a truly well-trained horse.

And wherein lies the correct execution of these three lessons? For the horse, as we have just explained, in correct footfall and activity of the back; for the rider, in correct seat and driving aids!

---

[72] *That to these three "causes" there also belong three parallel "effects" for neck-and-head position—namely: 1. a deep nose, 2. increased contact, and 3. a "rounded neck"—is self-evident for the average horse, of which alone there can be talk in such general discussions.*

Do the designations of the lessons indicate this with their bridle reference? If I may say so, do they not point almost to the opposite? Do they not involuntarily awaken the idea that in the working of neck and head lies the essence of the lesson, the essence of the aids, in the rein effect?

Added to this is that the course of development of theory in itself has already given this pernicious idea a special impetus. Today's views are based more or less on Seidler, the founder of straightening from depth, the first trailblazing opponent of high elevation. In his latter capacity, Seidler was permitted to seek unrestrainedly the quintessence of all riding in work at the neck, because high elevation with violent driving-together of back and hindquarters prevailed; that at that time a rider might claim these parts too little was out of the question. The counter-stroke did not fail to appear; one finally ended with "work from front to backend."

This error has indeed been recognized, and in principle today "work from behind to front" stands in force. But the Seidlerian ideas, which for their time quite rightly pushed neck work into the foreground, still have roots today in the riding world. In contrast to this, as Seidler—as opponent of excessive driving of the hindquarters—assigned neck work first place in every lesson, so today work from behind to front must remain clearly and unmistakably recognizable even in the smallest detail. To the natural ease which the Seidler tradition lends to neck work, a counterweight must be given; otherwise only a small minority believes in the grave opposition into which modern horsemanship has placed itself relative to earlier modes of thought.

How many riders might sign theses such as the following: "At the cross (seat) one pushes a resisting horse off, at the hand this effect only comes to expression!"—"At the loins / lower back / seat (Kreuz) one pushes a resisting horse off, at the hand this effect only comes to expression!"—"Only with the loins / lower back / seat (Kreuz) can one keep a stumbling horse on its legs; every rein aid only makes it stumble all the more!"—"From behind one can place a horse right or left; the hand only takes the effect!"—"A puller can only be held with the loins / lower back / seat (Kreuz); the more the rein intervenes, the more wildly he runs!" —And yet all these theses, though somewhat coarse, are entirely logical consequences of work from behind to front.

For the training of others—in contrast to the practical-theoretical study of the thinking, passionate rider—we encounter, however, still far more dangerous enemies, namely deeply rooted theoretical views. These are those of the recruit's instinct and the natural conception which the half-finished rider, the average of our remount riders, tends to have of mastering his horse. Every recruit sees in the rein, out of instinct and self-preservation, his natural means of rescue; every rider not already far advanced believes he should control his horse with the rein. A deficiency of rein aids we truly need not fear!

If instruction—the track theory, so to speak—is to have a chance of even approximately achieving correct proportions, it must, in opposition to these natural drives of the pupils, even denounce the rein and elevate the driving aids to the skies.

Written theory will have to avoid such extremes; but it must allow its great, so true principle—that neck-and-head position arises from orderly footfall and the correct form of the spinal column—to shine through all stages of training and through the most insignificant details.

To this would belong, for example, that in the description of every lesson, first gait, footfall, and activity of the back would be described, and only then, building upon this, neck-and-head position would be portrayed. Likewise, the aids which the rider must give for the execution of a lesson would have to be stated in the same sequence: first the seat and leg aids, then only the eventual aids of the hand. Every lesson would have to begin in motion, where seat and leg aids alone come effectively into play, and only then be permitted to stand still, when the horse also allows itself to be held from behind at the halt through light aids. In describing the errors that occur in the various lessons, those of footfall would first have to be dealt with; only then could those appearing at neck and poll be addressed; at the same time the latter would have to be traced back to the then still faulty footfall, etc.

Would not a very great step toward this goal be taken if an entirely new terminology were created, which for each lesson—indeed for every relationship between rider and horse—offered a designation derived from the function of the back and the hindquarters?

Would not the riding teacher be preserved from confusing cause, origin, and effect? Would not the learning rider, through the indication already contained in the command, be compelled to think more correctly and to work more precisely by directing his attention to the center of gravity of the lesson? Would not everyone who has to judge a movement or a horse under the rider be forced to direct his attention to the true criterion of training—the gait and the calmness in the horse?

Certainly! For theory itself would be unable to avoid, first, tracing the fundamental lines of the system more sharply and more intelligibly, and then building further upon these firm foundations in such a way that the style in which the whole is conceived would be reflected even in the smallest articulation of the instructional structure.

As a test, one need only attempt oneself to find a designation for the expression "to be on the bit" that corresponds to the principle of "work from behind toward the front." One will soon notice how difficult this is, and how intimately this concept is connected with the entire essence of the art of riding. For the earnestly inquiring mind is here compelled into chains of thought that encompass virtually all areas of the art of riding.

To indicate only a few things: the good jockey, the good hunting rider, the good campaign rider, the good school rider—all have their horse on the bit, and yet—what differences in form, posture, and style of movement! What contrasts (in truth only apparent, since there is only one art of riding) in the manner of riding the horse! Where lies the common element, where the distinction?—Or: the best-ridden horse is on the bit, but no less so is the horse that has only just been backed!—Or: what does the judgment about a trained horse mean: "it is brilliant on the bit"? Is this a permanent quality inherent in the animal, or does it disappear the moment in which the reins are confidentially laid upon the horse's neck?

Before these and a thousand other questions have become inwardly clear to the concerned person, no one will be permitted to venture to propose a new designation. Presumably there exists a full and entirely essence-reflecting expression for the wonderfully multifaceted condition of the horse that one is accustomed to describe as *"being on the bit"*[73] has become accustomed to it, not at all; perhaps it might finally even impose itself to decompose the concept itself into several others.

Be that as it may, one thing may already now be confidently prophesied:

"The definition of this still unnamed concept will continually require certain words again and again, certain words to be used rarely and only incidentally." To that category belong, in reference to the horse: *"balance, position of the center of gravity, looseness, throughness, impulsion and carrying power of the hindquarters, rounding of the back"*—in reference to the rider: *"looseness, harmonizing one's own center of gravity with that of the horse (seat of balance), purposeful allowing of one's own center of gravity to step out of the balance seat (weight aids), support (thus not constraint!) by means of leg and spur aids."*

To the latter category belong: neck, head, and poll, and, respectively, hand, rein, bit; of these this definition will have little to say.

Any further delving into this question is impossible here; it can only be discussed on the broadest possible basis. So that we do not appear to give stones instead of bread when we refer to it only briefly here, we wish merely to show that even a transformation of the technical terms would represent a significant advance—consider finally the lesson "bending" or "breaking" as an illustrative example! Let one call it: "shoulder-in-like bending" or "trot-like bringing-under of a hind leg." [74]

Could the lessons be described at all under these names without giving first place—and in particularly emphatic fashion—to the activity of the back and hindquarters, to the effect through weight and leg? Would it be conceivable that someone would wish to begin them on the spot? Could rider, instructor, or critical observer be in doubt for even a moment as to where the actual focal point of the lesson lies? Would one not rather have to see the principle of "work from behind toward the front" in every letter that theory writes down, in every word spoken in the arena—penetrating and resounding throughout?

---

[73] *Editor's note. On the true content of this concept, see p. 77.*
[74] *That this lesson can and must be ridden only with the horse placed into balance (thus with a lowered nose) is self-evident. The complete looseness of any lesson before the foundation (balance, throughness, beginning of back rounding and thereby a low nose) is thoroughly established must be emphasized with particular sharpness.*

That after these expectations, which were tied to the appearance of the Plinzner system, the disappointment was all the greater cannot be denied.

The occasion to take a position, however, did not arise until an article in no. 20 of the "Militär-Wochenblatt" (1892) pointed out, in our opinion, the serious danger of a victory of the new system over the already-institutionalized *Riding Instruction*. We set down our principal objections in the subsequent article in no. 40 of the "Militär-Wochenblatt" (1892):

The Steinbrecht–Plinzner Riding and Dressage System and Riding Instruction

The article published under the same title in no. 20 of the "Militär-Wochenblatt" allows the possibility that riding instruction might be reshaped in the sense of the new system to appear more clearly on the horizon. It therefore seems time to express those objections which may be raised against it, or against its conception.

What the new system seeks to achieve is both outstandingly correct and timely. What it will achieve, when it has become riding instruction and is passed on not by the inventor himself or by an enthusiastic, capable adherent, but by average instructors to average riders, will—according to our conviction—not be anything better than before.

We base ourselves here on the historical development of riding theory. No system of the past has been spared being misunderstood, and we believe that the new system is already here and there being misunderstood.

The high elevation of the old school, Seidler's elevation from depth, even Baucher's method—almost universally decried among us as the greatest charlatanry—all wanted, when correctly understood, exactly the same thing; all have, when correctly applied, shown great success.

If nevertheless one of these systems gave way to another, this lay solely in the fact that its true core was no longer correctly recognized. Every new system owes its origin primarily to the circumstance that the originally correct fundamental idea of the preceding system was increasingly misinterpreted over time, until finally these misunderstandings grew so excessive that practical results failed to appear and a reorganization became necessary. In the struggle of opinions, as is usual, the child was then thrown out with the bathwater; the old system was made so thoroughly bad that everything healthy contained within it vanished from the picture.

That this latter could happen shows clearly how little it has yet succeeded in unambiguously defining the deepest essence of the art of riding. For since rider and horse today still have the same anatomical construction as at the time of the old systems, and the laws of balance have likewise undergone no change, the deepest essence of riding must still remain the same.

All the misinterpretations which the past systems have had to endure therefore stem solely from the fact that the fundamental basis of all relationships between rider and horse was not thoroughly established. Mostly, the essence of the new system was to be designated by some catchword (high elevation, etc.), without, however, the inner content, the true significance of this word, having been surrounded by an unassailable barrier of objective justification—so that misunderstanding could not creep in.

Nor has the "unconditional collection" of the new system escaped misinterpretation. Despite the so frequent warning that the low forehand is only the preliminary stage, that the true essence of the system is instead to be sought in the engagement of the hindquarters, it is to be feared—indeed almost with certainty expected—that horses low in front and high behind will appear everywhere where average riders are trained under average instructors according to the new system.

For no rider drives by nature; every rider holds by nature. This unfortunately undeniable fact will, in our view, become a dangerous pitfall for the new system. Even among riders who possess full understanding of the new method of dressage, the great majority do not have at their disposal the sum of driving aids required in order, despite the low forehand, to assign the load to the hindquarters in appropriate measure. Even more, however, it is to be feared that the continual emphasis on "unconditional collection" will further intensify among the great mass of our riders the already naturally present inclination to be too active with the hand and too little with the driving aids—and thereby make correct dressage impossible.

The question now arises whether this danger cannot be eliminated.

First of all, it would seem advisable to replace the expression "unconditional collection," which repeatedly threatens to instinctively entice the rider to the use of the hand, with another one; it appears as though the designation "unconditional throughness" would not only remove the stimulus, but also more precisely represent the concept which the new system connects with "unconditional collection."

Above all, however, it would be necessary to pursue the fundamental conception upon which the entire relationship between rider and horse must be built—not only in the new system, but in every system—to its ultimate and deepest point of origin. Naturally, this can only occur on the broadest possible basis. Here, space permits only a brief indication.

For the mastery of the horse by the rider, collection is indeed the decisive point, and the correct solution of this question solves all riddles of riding. Until now, in all systems, including the new one, the hand appears to be the more or less important point for this. In truth, however, the hand has almost nothing to do with collection; rather, it is based upon those changes which arise in the horse through driving aids, namely:
1. in its balance,
2. in the coordination of its musculature.

With regard to the former, the well-known axiom of action and reaction comes into play here, specifically in the form: every organized body seeks to regain the innate, natural load-bearing relationship of its parts when this has been altered by external influence.

If therefore the rider drives the hindquarters under his weight and maintains the previous tempo through the reins with slight cooperation of the hand, he gives the horse an impulse—derived with natural necessity from the aid—to bring neck and head into a low position. A horse that is truly in balance in its tempo and momentary posture (this is the true meaning of correct "natural tempo") resembles a finely balanced scale, in which even a slight additional load on one pan suffices to cause the other, through a changed position, to undertake the redistribution of weight—i.e., for the horse to collect itself independently.

That this aid is no mere plaything, but rather in certain cases has an outright positively compelling character, becomes clear when one applies it, in a rapidly escalating manner, to a ridden horse stubbornly resisting collection. The more one on the spot drives the hindquarters under the hand that yields to every stiffening of the horse, the more forcefully it presses downward into the reins—and all the more so the higher and lighter the hand stands, the more powerfully the spur drives the hindquarters under, the more decisively the seat restrains the already engaged hindquarters. (This is the true meaning of elevation.)[75] Here one recognizes quite plainly how the hand in fact has almost nothing to do with collection; for on the spot it is felt most clearly how it is actually only the seat that pins the horse down, making any forward escape impossible.

At the same time, in such a horse one unmistakably recognizes the second effect brought about by the driving aids, namely that upon the musculature of the horse—something for which observing the elevation in front of a mirror is recommended. As soon as the horse, after some resistance, obeys the spur and steps under with the hindquarters, the back arches, and immediately the horse's natural striving begins to assert itself: to carry this arching forward, to let the neck also participate—briefly: to collect itself.

This second effect must, moreover, be a priori self-evident to every adherent of the new system; for it is merely the reversal of the previously asserted, purely anatomical and entirely unassailable proposition: *"Contact creates elevation of the back."*

The difference between the two conceptions is, however, from the equestrian standpoint a significant one—indeed, a principled one. In the one case, the enduring effect of the displacement of weight toward the hindquarters acts in the same direction; it too imperatively demands contact. The effect of weight is the truly operative factor; on the basis of the immutable laws of equilibrium it produces contact. The effect upon the musculature is merely a secondary influence, even if a highly welcome one and indispensable for later stages of dressage. In the other case, this decisive effect of weight is lacking—not in practice, when a master is in the saddle, but certainly in theoretical justification. For here the engagement of the hindquarters must

---

[75] *An elevation such as that presupposed in lines 5 to 3, col. 554 in no. 20 of the "Militär-Wochenblatt" is naturally meant neither here nor ever in riding instruction. Neither does the seat disturb the rounding of the back, nor the hand the collection; in particular, the latter absolutely does not wish to raise the neck, but merely sets the directional point for the engagement of the hindquarters higher and thereby promotes their loading, which—balanced forward—is precisely the true, natural source of collection.*

necessarily be left out of consideration, since it of itself already produces elevation of the back. Theoretically, therefore, only the proposition remains that contact alone creates elevation of the back.

This development leads us to the actual dividing line between the riding instruction and the new system. The differences cited by the article in No. 20 are, in our view, relatively secondary. The decisive point of opposition lies in the fact that the riding instruction regards equilibrium (purely physically speaking, see p. 17 § II) as the α and ω of dressage, and demands muscular engagement and collected posture of the horse only to the degree that can be achieved while maintaining equilibrium. The new system, conversely, takes the correct interweaving of the muscular framework as the α and ω of dressage and tacitly presupposes that the driving aids of the rider are powerful enough to maintain equilibrium in and despite the collected posture. With good riders, both systems are entirely equivalent. There it will be possible to increase the degree of collection to the highest level while preserving equilibrium. Here, conversely, the driving aids will nevertheless succeed, even with all the collection, in maintaining equilibrium. Nevertheless, equilibrium must always be preserved. With less capable riders, however, the relationship will shift substantially in favor of the riding instruction. With it we will indeed produce less highly collected horses, but in this modest degree of collection the horses will possess true equilibrium. The new system will produce excessively collected horses whose load distribution between forehand and hindquarters does not correspond, i.e., without equilibrium. Without this, however, no living, moving being can exist.

The calls for improvement and reform of the riding instruction are therefore, in our view, justified only in a formal sense. In substance it remains, as before, the best we have. An unfortunate coincidence caused the establishment of the concept of the "riding gait" through v. Hollenuffer and v. Oettingen to come somewhat too late for practical use in riding instruction; had it already been common property of the equestrian world at that time, a later, more concise presentation would have been possible—especially with regard to the significance of the muscular engagement of the horse.

To introduce this concept into the army and, based upon it, to derive every relationship between rider and horse solely from the two great factors that unify all forms and systems of horsemanship into a universal "natural" riding—namely, 1. the natural laws of equilibrium, and 2. the natural, innate muscular and skeletal formation of the horse—would indeed have been a significant step forward. Many individual matters would also have been resolved more satisfactorily in the process. Above all, this striving for a natural foundation would finally clarify the still obscure question of the hard and stiff side of the horse and its significance for dressage. In this, after all, lies the practical core of dressage; without a theory that soberly and clearly presents the inner connection between this peculiarity of the horse and the rider's aids conditioned by it, practice remains valueless and unused. Be that as it may, the riding instruction would have had no need to abandon any of its fundamental principles, nor to add anything previously lacking.

The same can scarcely be said of the new system. Rather, it builds its internal justification almost exclusively upon the second of the two pillars of riding instruction—the muscular engagement of the horse, the conditions for the riding gait as outstanding as the justification is in this sense, and as thoroughly all the conditions of the horse carrying the rider have been thought through and expressed in this direction, a certain one-sidedness necessarily adheres to the new system.

We can only briefly indicate here that everything connected with the conditions of equilibrium—such as natural tempo (cf. note to p. 99 of Vol. II of the riding instruction), appropriate elevation (see above), weight aids, etc.—has not received full consideration. We would emphasize, however, that even the concept of the riding gait itself begins to take on a one-sided form in the new system.

It is by no means necessary that a horse stand low in front in order to be a riding-gait horse, as even less knowledgeable adherents of the new system often seem to believe. In strong gaits, which require a far-forward center of gravity, this is indeed necessary for every horse, including the cavalry horse. If a horse cannot do this, its training is not correct. For otherwise it would move in an equilibrium unsuitable for the required performance. But the same horse must equally be able, for collected gaits, to shift its center of gravity backward by thrust from the hindquarters (self-carriage) and also significantly withdraw the forehand. Otherwise, the center of gravity would again be unsuitable for the required performance. The muscular tension of back and hindquarters would have to be enormously greater than with a naturally appropriate center-of-gravity position. For certain horses (weak-backed ones) this may be a blessing; for most, an exercise to be employed here and there with advantage—but as a norm and ultimate goal hardly acceptable! For in the end all factors for the gait should be utilized in such a way that the movement remains elastic (riding gait), while at the same time sparing the horse's strength (most favorable center-of-gravity position). Here too we see the conditions of equilibrium recede behind the effort to find the entire essence of horsemanship in muscular engagement.

We cannot regard this as correct; rather, we believe that a universal justification of gait and aids, one that accounts for all equestrian phenomena, can only be achieved by constantly returning to the laws of equilibrium. It cannot suffice to think only of individual elements of equilibrium, of center-of-gravity position; rather, it is necessary to regard this, together with the skeletal and muscular configuration that produces the riding gait, as the two cornerstones of the entire doctrinal structure. Only in this way can every movement of the horse, every influence of the rider, be clearly recognized as the natural consequence of these two eternal, immutable conditions for the horse carrying a rider.

Only thus can correct conceptions of the essence of horsemanship—unclouded by misunderstandings and false interpretations—be made accessible even to the great majority.

***

All later softening of the original demands, which were intended to make the Plinzner system more acceptable, could not change the initial opinion that it was not called upon to replace the riding instruction. The standpoint of the latter has, however, undeniably shifted. Not only has the forward-inclined seat been abandoned; even the "unconditional contact" itself has been strongly weakened in its significance—at least by friends of the system (articles in Nos. 30 and 31 of the "Militär-Wochenblatt" 1900).

It was overlooked that a firmly constructed, internally coherent system—and this is a quality the Plinzner system possesses to a high degree—cannot accept foreign elements without abandoning itself. A logically constructed system cannot be patched. *Sit ut est, aut non sit!* [Let them be as they are, or not at all!] In the articles of the Wochenblatt it even came to a direct contradiction: "The cornerstone of the system is deep contact; but—it is secondary."

To clarify this, the following article finally appeared in No. 56 of the "Militär-Wochenblatt" 1900:

Reply to: "The Plinzner System and Cavalry Riding"

Motto: No horse in the world can be ridden without auxiliary reins; one must never be missing—the spur!

Judgments about the Plinzner system are gradually beginning to clarify. An obvious adherent of the Plinzner system concludes an article in Nos. 30/31 of the "Militär-Wochenblatt" with regret that secondary matters cause the main issue to be forgotten: after all, it is entirely irrelevant whether the neck is somewhat higher or lower, the nose somewhat sharper or less sharply presented, provided only that suppleness is present!

A more accurate remark can scarcely be made—but a harsher condemnation of the Plinzner system can hardly be conceived. The author forgets that it is not the Plinzner system that is the suffering party, to which malicious opponents wish to deny contact. Rather, intolerance lies on the side of the Plinzner system, which, instead of the self-development demanded, for example, by the friends of the riding instruction—whose capacity for improvement in other directions is by no means denied—for the neck and head position of each individual horse, wants to prescribe deep contact once and for all as the ultimate goal.

One could still live peacefully with this demand, for the great majority of horses will find themselves in full contact even with methods other than that advocated by the Plinzner system. But the path by which the goal is to be reached is equally strictly confined and schematized. The horse is to enter deep contact as soon as possible and then remain in it permanently.

Here, however, a wide rift opens between the entire conceptual approach of the Plinzner system and the view represented by the motto of this article.

For this apparently paradoxical statement is meant in earnest. It is intended to say that every attempt to obtain contact through the hand is incorrect.

Contact is therefore achieved in another way! What, then, is it really?

There are many ways in which it can be obtained, many ways in which it can be explained—but only one correct one.

"It is that balancing of weight which the horse voluntarily and independently performs forward-and-downward, when the rider's aids succeed—through driving and engaging the hindquarters beneath the elastic rider's center—while maintaining light, elevated, and ever-yielding connection with the still unresolved musculature of the neck and poll, to produce a substantially greater loading of the hindquarters than that innate to the horse." [76]

That is the significance of contact for theory, whose task it is to uncover the anatomical-physiological connections between rider and horse.

What, then, is it for the horse? Evidently its first base, with which it meets the rider in order to accept the loading of the hindquarters, which later expands into lateral bending.

What is it finally for the rider? Initially, confirmation that his influence from behind is effective; then the electrical signal for seat and spur either not to allow the balancing at all, or only to a measured degree, or—for the hand— to oppose skillfully and from the correct place in order either to prevent completely the lowering of neck and head (true relative elevation, which is of course permissible only in later stages), or to allow it partially, whether forward, forward-downward, or downward, whereby the neck governs the length of stride.

Whether this is achieved without strengthening the contact—by stretching (release of still hardened neck muscles)—or by connection between hand and bit (contact), or by yielding at the poll with only minimal lowering of the neck (correct contact), varies.

In a word: this manner of establishing contact is not a working of the neck in the narrow sense, but rather initiates the working of the whole horse, as a unity created by nature, from the very first attempts at its shaping. It skillfully balances the weight of the hindquarters against that of the forehand, leads to better equilibrium, increased bending of the hindquarters, release of hardened muscular areas, contact, elevation—briefly, everything that dressage requires, coming from the very first attempts at shaping.

---

[76] *Space requires brevity. Interested readers are therefore referred to No. 40 of the "Militär-Wochenblatt" of 1892, where this thesis is indeed justified—if only aphoristically, yet still in a more detailed manner. Here, only a few questions illuminating the tendency are posed:*
"How many minutes can a miller's apprentice, even one of extraordinary strength, carry a 1-hundredweight sack of flour in an upright posture, without being forced into a forward inclination of the body?"
"How long can a brewer carry a fifty-liter keg in front of himself without leaning backward?"
"How long can a maidservant hold a bucket of water in her right hand without lateral inclination?"
And finally, as the last question: "How long can a horse endure a similar overloading of the hindquarters, without being forced into a redistribution of weight forward or downward?"

Which of these dressage advances is to be promoted in a specific case remains a matter of feel, which must decide in which direction the horse is momentarily most in need.

And how economical this work is![77] Once the interplay of weights is set in motion, the rider has literally only to do exactly what a child playing with a scale does: from time to time "tap one pan"—but not, like the child, with the hand, but with the spur; and not arbitrarily either pan, but only the rear one.

And how intensive this work is! The rider always gains something: if the balancing of weight is not allowed, good—then the load increases behind; or it is partially allowed, then the hand sets the excess weight swinging into the forehand into some previously named neck work, etc. But not through heavy resistance; rather through correct height of position and, in emergencies, lightning-fast and immediate release. In this way it remains independent, since it skillfully avoids the resistance of the musculature so long as this is still hardened.

Only one error is conceivable in this conception of the transformation of the horse's body—namely, permitting the full balancing of weight sought by the horse, the acceptance of full contact in depth.

The scale swings only so long as the horse is more heavily loaded behind than innately; if, by allowing full or even increased balancing of weight, the rear pan is relieved, the scale stands still, with excess weight settling forward.

It is an almost Mephistophelian thought: precisely that innate quality of the horse which it seems to bring with it as an inconvenience for the rider—the natural greater loading of the forehand and the immanent striving of the horse continually to regain it—is to be exploited as the chief, indeed the sole, means for dressage and subjugation of the horse.

If it did not exist, it would have to be created retroactively by nature for the rider. For without it, the horse would indeed, as certain theorists wish to make plausible in the case of direct bending of the hindquarters, be able to creep together behind. With correct driving this is simply a physical impossibility (see Chapter Eight).

After all this, we not only cannot approve the standpoint of the Plinzner system, but we even perceive the greatest obstacle to "absolute" contact (contact with the ancillary conditions demanded in the explanation: lateral bending, riding gait, spring renewed from stride to stride, thrust, etc.) precisely in deep contact from the outset.

---

[77] *The incredible effortlessness is very noteworthy. I personally have, on my inspection days in the officers' riding division, frequently mounted eight to ten horses in succession. The work naturally took place within, and not beyond, the highest collection still possible for the horses, since the sole purpose consisted in correcting faulty horses. As a rule, there was no perspiration on the rider; the horses, however, although each stood at my disposal for only five to six minutes, were always very warm. Naturally, such work can only be done with the spur, which costs nothing—just like the rider's own weight and that of the horse.*

The same gentleman who supplied the motto of this article as a judgment on auxiliary reins gave, immediately after the appearance of the Plinzner system, his vote as follows: "In many details impeccable! In principle: Seidler *redivivus* [reborn]! Work from front to back!"

We stand with regard to deep contact as the beginning of work in such a way that we can have it at any moment—for the horse strives toward it unceasingly, even greedily with somewhat sharper spur work—but we guard against accepting more of it than is required to ensure contact, thrust into the hand, yielding at the poll and mouth, because it presents itself to us as the horse's strongest basis against loading of the hindquarters.

Unfortunately, this point is not the only one on which we disagree with the Plinzner system.

Since neck and back, for a faultless theory, are merely parts of the same spinal column delivered as a unified whole by nature, whose positions mutually condition one another, it is clear that differences must also exist with regard to the riding gait if one takes such a position on the neck and head.

I shall be brief. Elevation plays a major role in the Plinzner system—and rightly so! But of lowering we hear almost nothing! And yet it too deserves careful attention. v. Hollenuffer, to whom we owe the theory of the riding gait, did not neglect it either. In the most convincing manner he explains that both activities, which together represent the "back oscillations," are indispensable for an elastic, spring-like gait. If lowering is absent or imperfect, the oscillations are lacking just as much as when elevation is not virtuously fluent in the horse.

Now, however, it is precisely the lower back muscles that are of almost superhuman strength. If we do not stretch these before we allow the entire muscular framework of the horse to spring against itself (collection), we will certainly suffer the consequences later.

According to our conviction, every resistance of the forehand has its cause only exceptionally there; rather, in almost all cases it lies in the back (incorrect muscular engagement) or in insufficient suppleness of the hindquarters (lack of equilibrium). Above all, the deficiency manifests itself in free gallop. Horses go in apparently flawless collected gallop; but as soon as the pace increases, the jumps lose their carrying quality, the nose begins to strike, the hand is burdened. Going forward (strong contraction of the lower muscles) functions well, but with the lowering of the back (strong stretching of the lower muscles) it fails.

If one absolutely wishes to find, at some particular place on the horse, the secret of mastering the horse in spite of its resistance, then I would propose, instead of every function derived from the neck, that of the back. It is not suppleness faultlessly regulated, i.e., it arches just as softly and elastically as it powerfully tightens, then the build may otherwise be whatever it will, the horse is supple and follows the lightest weight aids (which are, after all, the only truly effective ones).

Plinzner System—Fillis—Natural Horsemanship

Who does not know horses with pronounced "deer necks" and very high croups,[78] but with faultless back mechanics and powerful loins, which are not only absolutely reliable, but also extremely comfortable hunting horses!

The matter is, in an equestrian sense, entirely clear! As soon as the hindquarters step under, the wonderfully strong back musculature of these horses draws the forehand toward the hindquarters and thereby prevents the rolling forward of the body. And just as well, stretching itself, it pushes the forehand elastically and without disturbance forward.

Nose, poll, neck are, so to speak, simply held; one must not pull on them nor press upon them. Then these horses immediately become rigid, never to be seen again.

These observations too must make one mistrustful of the Plinzner system. Where collection is demanded before the muscles have been loosened, there is almost always, among average riders and horses with stronger backs, pulling.

It is therefore regrettable that the Plinzner system contains an obvious gap precisely at this point. Admittedly, a closer explanation and justification of the conditions for flexion would scarcely have produced results favorable to "the bridle at any price."

Besides these two pillars of riding art, balance and correct muscular engagement, there exists yet a third: "the innate crookedness of the horse."

Correctly used, it offers the possibility of meeting the forward drive of the horse without disturbance of the swinging of the back, and thus relatively comfortably and through, if the hindquarters powerfully spring into the restraining hands.

Every good jockey and steeplechase rider, and likewise every better breaker of a sales stable exploits it practically in this sense. But theory still stands for the moment alien to it. Nor has its nature yet been explained, nor the utilization of this peculiarity of the horse for dressage clarified.

For systems which rest upon conditions of balance, the great deficiency which this represents does not come so sharply to expression, because here the momentarily resisting hind leg is always first brought up before the opposing hand demands throughness. Nevertheless, even here only the correct use of crookedness permits the horse to be kept with the most playful aids and thereby, despite the sharpest driving behind, to remain light in front.

For a system, however, which, like the Plinzner system, is constructed in the first instance upon correct muscular engagement, the doctrine of the crookedness of the horse is absolutely essential.

---

[78] *Standing spectators at the Baden races may recall on this occasion Omnium II by Upas out of Bluette, one of the most marvelous gallopers France has ever produced. That he was a back-pacer of the first rank will scarcely be doubted by anyone who saw him go down the course with that leap, powerful though unpleasant for the patriotic spectator, which is accustomed to distinguish the representatives of the Republic. Nevertheless he stood very high in the gallop, the nose almost horizontal. His experienced trainer, however, carefully refrained from touching this.*

To discuss it here, there is no space. Only this may be said: that the first conduct of the rider corresponds exactly to that of the cyclist whose handlebars are set crooked. He leaves the crookedness; then the thrust of the rear wheel, despite the faulty alignment, goes directly and unhindered to the front wheel.

How the transformation takes place in the horse, how active utilization then occurs through dressage, that to explain clearly is possible only on a very broad basis.

Touched upon, however, the question has indeed been!

First by Mr. von Oettingen in his spirited and astonishingly sharply conceived brochure, *Über die Geschichte und die verschiedenen Formen der Reitkunst* [On the History and the Various Forms of the Art of Riding], the only equestrian book known to me since von Holleuffer that is furnished with new and logically developed ideas. Then, and here more tangibly, by Mr. von Reudell in a remark on Chapter II of the stimulating Whyte-Melville *Reitererinnerungen* [Riding Reminiscences.] He indicates quite definitely and aptly on which side one must first take hold and how one must proceed approximately further. However, as is to be expected with a mere remark, everything is only indicated in rudimentary fashion.

The new edition of the Plinzner system likewise contains, according to the announcement of the article in No. 31 of the "Militär-Wochenblatt," a special chapter on this matter. From the communications about its main points, which the title certainly makes reliable, it emerges, however, that qualitatively nothing new is brought.

"Side issues," therefore, are by no means what separate us from the Plinzner system. We find rather, at each of the three cornerstones upon which the entire dressage rests, strong and principled contradictions to our conception of the relationships between rider and horse.

***

Against the aims of the Plinzner system, the *Natural Horsemanship* therefore turns scarcely—only by further individualization—at all! The path toward these aims, however, as well as the entire conceptual framework, is fundamentally different!

How the *Natural Horsemanship* relates to riding instruction emerges equally unambiguously from the article of the year 1892.

The principles coincide throughout. The formal capacity for improvement of riding instruction is, of course, self-evident in a book that stands on the threshold of celebrating its twenty-fifth anniversary and has lived through a period that, in figures such as v. Holleuffer, v. Oettingen, Plinzner, Fillis, saw at work more leading authorities—partly as sharp thinkers, partly as first-rate practical riders—than almost any other century. In which direction this formal improvement would be considered advantageous is stated in essence both in the article of 1886 and in that of 1892.

And now finally, the position of the *Natural Horsemanship* in relation to Fillis!

Without the article of the year 1892 it would be in a bad position! The explanation given there of the origin of the bit contact (with Fillis called "*flexion directe*," cf. the note on page 65 of his work, or "releasing of the bit," cf. page 72) through "energetic driving forward with seat and spur under the high, light, yielding hand (this is the true meaning of collection)" sees its collection[79]—which always includes "*flexion directe*," "releasing of the bit"—so despairingly similar that it would be inconceivable if it were now only just being expressed, perhaps unconsciously, but nevertheless appearing as suggested by Fillis.

But Fillis' work fortunately did not appear until 1894, and since that explanation in the *Natural Horsemanship*, as with Fillis (cf. Preface, page XI), is the cornerstone and foundation of the entire conception, not only the independence of this individual exposition but of the *Natural Horsemanship* in its entirety is proven, as well as the complete agreement with Fillis in principle.

That the *Natural Horsemanship* speaks of bitting, Fillis of collection, is no contradiction.[80] What they have in common is this: "The driving," as the former says, "the impulsion," as the latter says, "works upon neck and poll!" (Chapter one of the *Natural Horsemanship*, the above-cited note on page 133 in Fillis), and further: "Never press the neck together!" says the *Natural Horsemanship*; "Let the nose come slightly forward!" says Fillis; "Then the forehand will adjust itself!" both say.

I would like, in the interest of Mr. Fillis, to emphasize on this occasion that his "collection" is almost always misunderstood. This lies in the fact that he suppresses the expression "bitting" in his vocabulary, as he states on page 158, lines 1 and 2, but under this "bitting" understands Baucher's deep bitting.

I would like, in the interest of Mr. Fillis, to emphasize on this occasion that his "uprighting" is almost throughout falsely understood. This is due to the fact that he literally says of the expression "bridling," as he does on page 158 lines 1 and 2, that he has "suppressed it in his vocabulary," but under this "bridling" he means Baucher's deep flexion.

In truth, his elevation always contains the fully complete ("high collection") or almost complete ("set in the hand") brought-up nose. He knows no elevation without "*flexion directe*" (= correct bridle contact = yielding exclusively at the poll) at all.[81] A single glance at the photographs proves this.

---

[79] Cf. especially the note on page 133 of Fillis' work: "I have already said that a high collection can only be achieved through impulsion from behind."

[80] *This rather proves how little accurate the misleading designations "collection" and "bitting" are with respect to the essence of the matter.*

[81] *How he thinks about the high nose-position = elevation without releasing the poll, he himself states on page 184, lines 3 to 6 of his work: "If the horse carries its head too high, one makes use of the curb reins. A head that is directed too high and backward damages the hindquarters." It goes without saying that the "Natural Horsemanship" also upholds the latter statement—only three times underlined—yet for it, as for Fillis, "not too high" is neither identical with "quite deep," nor is a "deep nose" identical with a "low forehand."*

Natural Horsemanship

In high collection the poll flexion is enormously high (especially Plate XXVII Fig. 2, Plate XXXI Fig. 2), but even in horses described merely as "set into the hand" it is still very strong. Only because the horses, through the enormous impulsion from behind, are at the same time raised so high, does the poll flexion appear smaller; if one were to lower them only halfway in the neck, without changing the angle of the lower neck/jaw, they would stand with completely vertical noses.

A difference, of course, exists between Fillis and the *Natural Horsemanship*. Both continually have entirely different aims! He has uninterrupted backward gallop on three legs and similar marvels as his ultimate goal before his eyes; on the other hand, *Natural Horsemanship* only a long, loose hunting gallop of often difficult horses under riders of average quality.

I do not wish to anticipate Mr. Fillis as to which height of the neck he would recommend if he wished only to achieve the latter; from my side, however, I can assure that although I would never presume to ride Fillis's methods myself, if I were ever to attempt it, my theory would nevertheless never allow me to arrive at any idea other than that of high elevation (naturally also including direct flexion).

We both work the horses by bringing the horse's weight under the high, light position, with the mouth merely felt, every backward effect—because it arrests impulsion—being carefully avoided by the hand (which for the uninitiated gives the impression of "elevation"), and we let the noses down when and insofar as it corresponds to our purpose: Fillis therefore never does so except for momentary highest collection; the *Natural Horsemanship* immediately does so whenever it believes it has sufficient advance in balance and engagement of the hindquarters in order to allow the horse to go forward without overbalancing.[82]

For this difference in handling there is yet another circumstance to be considered, namely the duration of the effort. Anyone who has seen Fillis ride will recall how after each performance he would suddenly release the reins onto the horse's neck out of the highest collection, and the horse would then move quietly, almost drowsily, like the oldest remount horse, going along in an extended outline.

In short, he demands the tremendous requirements of impulsion and carrying power of the hindquarters from the horse only for moments, while we wish to canter for twenty minutes and longer. It is self-evident that, out of consideration for the duration of the work, we allow the horse to settle into its natural, innate balance, into a wider and deeper frame. But note well: to allow it to settle, not to press the horse into it. We permit the supple horse to take on a limited deeper position for recovery or longer endurance; but we never force the resistant horse into it by hand.

---

[82] *i.e., with a good rider, even with difficult horses, mostly in a few minutes; with a moderately skilled rider, depending on circumstances, in 8 to at most 14 days.*

Incidentally, I am by no means a blind admirer of Fillis. I even consider his theoretical justification in many respects to be directly incorrect. (For this, however, his presentation of pure fact—especially concerning collection and rider's tact—is unsurpassed and magnificent; his personal riding lies beyond all imagination!) I wish only to emphasize two particularly striking and, for campaign riding, significant points: his views 1. on obedience and 2. on the horse's memory.

What Fillis calls disobedience is nothing more than the still-existing inability of the horse's musculature to perform what is demanded without strong discomfort. The horse does not become disobedient; rather, given the speed with which Fillis advances the work, it must become disobedient—or more correctly, must express pain. I have observed this, even in very willing, compliant horses, precisely when applying certain Fillisian aids of enormous effect—to which I shall return—up to the point of certainty. Not only the point of collection at which so-called "disobedience" appears, but also the manner in which it expresses itself, I can predict almost invariably in horses with which I work continuously, with positive certainty, even when they are only momentarily ridden by others.

It must come to this if I truly raise the demand to that point: conflict is then, by necessity of nature, present.

I speak of this only because Fillis generally recommends conflict urgently. From his standpoint he is entirely right. With his secure seat, his energy and his routine, even in the highest excitation of the horse, to prevent any damage to the horse or to himself, he may fight without concern; and he must do so given the colossal demands he places upon collection, suppleness, and correct shaping of even the smallest muscular ramifications. Without embittered conflict—though not embitterment—he cannot reach his goals.

For us campaign riders this applies only very limitedly. Personally, I am a great friend of conflict. I very often mount disobedient service horses or those of comrades and then find myself in the same position as Fillis: to enforce things in a few minutes which a calm dressage would require just as many weeks to achieve. Likewise, as a teacher, I compel every insufficiently active rider toward his training through the demand for increased collecting aids leading to a gentle conflict. Finally, I am fully aware that difficult conformations cannot be brought into form without conflict.

But—with the exception of my own struggles with already disobedient horses—the assessment of the situation is for me exactly the opposite of Fillis'.

For the riders instructed by me, "disobedience," and thus a reason for "conflict" in the Fillisian sense, does not exist at all. Rather, it is solely a matter of eliminating the resistance which the musculature, crowded by increased collection, naturally opposes to the rider's aids. Thus there must be no talk of anger or irritation on the rider's part, just as little as of any intention to thoroughly punish the disobedient animal—something to which the rider tends all the more the less capable he is.

No! The entire conception must be exactly that of a physician who, for example, restores natural function to a foot joint stiffened after a fracture by means of movement exercises. Without approaching the boundary where strong discomfort, even moderate pain, occurs, he will not achieve healing; but he would be inhumane if he misinterpreted the poor patient's grimacing or other pain expressions and intensified his demands further. Rather, the sensible physician will indeed approach the boundary of tolerable pain as closely as possible, but never cross it. He will further approach this boundary only gradually, act upon it as gently as possible, and finally not work continuously upon it alone, but intermittently apply milder influence and from time to time pause altogether.

Exactly so must the rider proceed. Here we stand in the midst of the conditions for success and failure of the entire dressage.

There are namely two erroneous paths, of which it is difficult to say which is worse either the instructor recoils as soon as the horse shows the slightest unrest and demands relaxation of the aids, or he "lets it go on," and the riding arena often resembles a tournament ground resounding with blows and thrusts.

The correct path lies precisely in the middle. Briefly stated, the rider must, under all circumstances, approach the boundary of strong discomfort for the horse, but must never cross it. This boundary is marked by striking, often very peculiar contortions of the croup, small canter bounds, light lifting of the forehand, restrained elevated stepping of the forelegs, and similar phenomena. Then it is time to measure the aids so finely and gently that they neither increase collection nor allow a weakening, but instead accompany the movements of the horse breathing-like (chapter seven), maintaining them at the same level.

At first, therefore, they will act lightly, as long as the horse does not yield to them; they will weaken more and more as soon as suppleness appears. After initially only a few (two to three), later several strides in this suppleness, follows yielding of the reins, praise, renewal of the demand, which then gradually increases in duration and degree.

One thing remains infinitely important here! The rider must approach this shaping with free disposition over all his aids…If the horse, through insufficient or excessive forward drive, leaning on the bit, etc., renders part of the aids ineffective (anatomically speaking: if the horse does not carry itself fully in balance under release of its muscles), then there can be no talk of fine intervention by the rider resembling that of a physician. The rider must sit upon the horse just as securely, freely, and masterfully as the physician stands at the bed or sofa beside the patient he is treating.

I recall here what was explained in chapter three regarding the average tension in the horse that produces the gait. This is the most important thing in almost the entire art of riding! Whoever already expends any active aids merely to maintain the gait will never count among the better riders. The gaits themselves—whether strong canter or shortened trot—must arise solely from the composition of the horse's spinal column according to strength and direction; the rider's aids participate only passively insofar as a certain weight effect, a certain seat pressure upon the spring of the back—in harmony with the gait being ridden—ensures balance. Only then are seat, leg, and hand available to the rider to shape this gait, self-generated by tone within the horse, according to need. Then, however, even the finest, almost imperceptible aids achieve noticeable effect.

Understood thus, "conflict" is the inexorable but measured enforcement of the rider's aids, adapted to the horse's sensitivity, an absolutely indispensable—indeed, one may say the sole—means for the education of both rider and horse.

We already mentioned in chapter seven that, according to our conception, the training of both coincides exactly; after achieving balance between rider and horse it consists in nothing more than the uninterrupted alternation between calm, undisturbed progression of horse- and rider-weight (self-carriage of the horse, balance-seat of the rider) and increase of collection or lateral suppleness through rapidly but precisely adapted aids growing up to the highest limit attainable without direct force.

We strive toward the final goal—quiet self-carriage of the horse under full obedience to the aids—from two ends, as it were. I do not hold much of the so-called "obedience exercises" as training means. With them it usually comes to uncontrolled conflict. They are then merely proof that blind obedience in the ordinary gaits was not demanded. Where this is demanded, they are merely "obedience tests" which are passed with brilliance.

The foundation of dressage upon the horse's memory sounds especially strange coming from a master such as Fillis, who in such admirable fashion understands how to subjugate even the smallest muscle of the horse and compel it to blind, machine-like obedience to his aids. Every single one of his own exquisitely fine descriptions of aids for his more complex school movements places him in the wrong in this respect. No—like a great organist, he draws certain registers, strikes the keys, and in harmonic flow the instrument gives forth the sound-flood, the horse reproduces the rhythm of the demanded gait. Therein lies precisely his entire unattainable greatness!

Everything that merely bears the appearance of obedience through memory instead of obedience to aids must be eradicated in the horse—and even more so in the rider. Much sinning still occurs here!

As soon as a higher degree of balance and suppleness has been achieved, I have riders work daily as oppositely as possible. Today the lesson begins with reins on the neck, tomorrow with sharpest collection; today with free canter, tomorrow with collection on the spot and subsequent lateral movements; today with entirely high, tomorrow with entirely deep carriage;[83] today with full seat

---

[83] *Only for better, individually selected riders or officers. In these moments full plucking occurs, in order to educate riders universally. After the hindquarters have become supple, this is also an exercise introduced with advantage for the horses. (For more see the conclusion of chapter four.)*

and inactive legs (seat aids only), tomorrow with inclined seat and replacement of the intentionally eliminated seat aids by leg or spur; Today the trot work with perceptibly the finest guidance, the horse remaining almost uninfluenced in the posture it has chosen for itself; tomorrow under careful pressing through of each individual step by means of the strongly elastic, resisting rein. Today with affectionate attention to the crookedness still present in the horse, accompanied by ever greater suppleness in the direction from back to front; tomorrow with intentional ignoring of it, whereby the suppleness of itself diminishes somewhat.

During the first three to four attempts the horses will also become somewhat restless in this work, particularly when one lets them count off in pairs and orders No. 1 to trot and No. 2 to gallop, and then vice versa; but obedience to the aids increases enormously.

For my taste, a training system that cannot begin the conclusion of training just as well with gallop and jumping in impeccable calm as with the popular schema is not fully trained. The campaign horse need not be able to do very much, but what it can do, it must be able to do at any time and under all circumstances.

These and other deficiencies in the theoretical foundation in Fillis, however, recede as entirely insignificant in comparison with the practical instruction he provides.

This applies above all to the rein contact characteristic of the French school—according to his own account not personally his, but generally belonging to it. On the other hand, its effect constitutes a brilliant illustration of our conviction that a sharp and precise theoretical grounding cannot be dispensed with in the art of riding; without it, the most valuable and best often remains hidden.[84]

When I first took up the Fillis work, I was, after a cursory perusal of the first hundred pages, almost more disappointed than after the appearance of Plinzner's system. The peculiar longeing or liberty work reminded me of the circus and seemed to me, just like the work in hand for campaign purposes, both too complicated and too refined, and therefore worthless. The role that memory appeared to play—trick-dressage instead of bodily control—was thoroughly unsympathetic to me; the idea of "placing the horse in balance by erecting the neck" (heading of his chapter beginning on page 76) stood in diametrical opposition to my demand that every function of the neck be explained theoretically as a direct consequence of the working of the hindquarters[85] and to proceed accordingly in practice, so much so that, even before I came to the "rein handling," I was full of prejudice. After this chapter, however, I said to myself: "Good heavens, how petty! The way the reins are taken up is really entirely irrelevant; what matters is only how one acts with them. Let the rider take them

---

[84] *I do not believe that anyone, by mere study of the Fillis work, would be able to recognize the type of rein handling as that which is precisely the most valuable for practical use.*
[85] *The frequently cited remark on page 133 of Fillis' work proves its exact agreement with this view; on page 76, only the expression is chosen incorrectly, as is almost unavoidable given the intimate connection between hindquarters and forehand and the now customary technical terminology.*

between his teeth if, in this way, he personally can handle them most smoothly and delicately!"

Only the later chapters, especially the fifteenth, allowed me to recognize the downright genius of the master. Nevertheless, in accordance with my overall conception of the worthlessness of any effect upon the forehand, the rein handling still appeared to me entirely a secondary matter.

Only practical experiment was to teach me better! Probably because the instinctive riding forward with a high carriage, in which the contact was at first intentionally not fully allowed, had long been familiar to me, I succeeded immediately in the correct application. What was remarkable, however, was that it happened to concern a quite conspicuously difficult horse, whose peculiar nature had, until then, seemed to allow me only to a limited degree the high carriage,[86] yet even under these circumstances, and although I rode only on a simple thick snaffle with double reins, the result—balance and correct engagement of the back musculature—was achieved as if by magic at a single stroke.

The upper rein of the right hand—I had chosen the handling shown in Plate X, Figure 2, *séparation du filet et du mors*—produced this; the lower reins nevertheless permitted, while maintaining balance, an effect upon the bars that produced contact.

Every attempt to press downward was prevented by a slight upward striving of the right hand; every attempt to remain "over" the hand was eliminated by a playful yielding of the lower reins.[87] After ten to twelve rapid successive alternations of these effects, the horse abandoned both attempts and for the first time truly placed itself at poll and hand.

In doing so, no aid was forced. On the contrary, the tendency toward a forward-leaning seat, which the sensitive back had always brought with it until then, vanished; the horse "set" the rider of its own accord. The weight shifted lightly backward (consequence of the stepping-under hindquarters), the seat rose slightly (consequence of the beginning rounding of the back, chapter three, especially the remark on page 59), the croup was unburdened (consequence of both factors); in short, I was completely master of my aids and thus of my horse.

What I had striven for in vain for weeks—under-loading the forehand, and the already deficient balance being entirely lost—disappeared. Every higher carriage once again burdened the back and caused unrest, strong physical

---

[86] *Thoroughbred mare, nervous and sensitive, built high behind, placed under herself in front, deep, for my weight too light a back, complete "deer-neck," completely horizontal nose, extremely sensitive mouth; shuffling trot steps and storming in the canter. Forcing collection according to my method was not difficult, but then she literally threw herself onto the forehand, and the balance, which was already deficient anyway, was completely lost. Every higher degree of collection in turn burdened the back and caused unrest.*

[87] *As will become evident from the course of the exposition, what is decisive here, naturally, is also the "driving," the "impulsion from behind."*

exertion—was achieved within three to four minutes without any expenditure of strength. Since the mare now allowed herself to be taken up with the lightest aids, the result of the first day was complete harmony between rider and horse in all gaits, which she acknowledged by contented snorting, especially in the canter, which I had entirely set aside since the beginning of arena work. The horse, too, was not particularly strained, in contrast to earlier days.

As gratifying as this practical result was, it was initially just as embarrassing to me as a counter-proof of my riding convictions. The neck therefore did indeed have a substantial share in regulating the gait!

In Fillis himself, however, no further instruction regarding the magical effect of his handling is to be found. The reason he gives—the higher position of the snaffle, the lower of the curb—even introduced new doubts. For even on a particularly difficult horse with a simple snaffle, the effect had emerged as evidently powerful.

Reassuring was only that Fillis himself, too, found the essence of the high carriage not in his handling, but in the impulsion from behind (see the oft-cited remark on page 133 in Fillis).

I, too, had felt this clearly in the practical experiment! For horse and rider alike, the essential changes occurred behind: there in the stepping-under of the hindquarters and the rounding of the back, here in the seat that had become independent of its own accord. Here too it remained valid: because the hindquarters push and carry, the back rounds and un-rounds, there occurs in front both taking-hold and pushing-off.

It could therefore only lie in the fact that the new handling made it possible to control the impulsion generated behind more securely, more precisely, and more variably.

And so it is indeed! The almost incomprehensible, irresistible effect of this handling upon first acquaintance is not only not a proof against our conception of the horse's movement, but rather a full confirmation of the Hollerith theory of back oscillations that is decisive for us.

One forgets again and again that these oscillations consist of successively following upward and downward arching of the back muscles, and that excessive arching is just as dangerous for the gait and especially for its control as excessive hollowing; that too weak a hollowing is just as paralyzing for the elasticity of the gait as too weak an arching. If we had a means that allowed us to regulate the degree of arching and hollowing, to diminish a plus, to increase a minus, then—if one recalls the mastery of the horse on the basis of back oscillations set out in chapter three—we would quickly and unfailingly be able to subject the horse to us.

Now—this means we have precisely in the Fillis handling, whose decisive moment lies not in the possibility of high elevation—this can also be produced with any other handling—but in the possibility, through arbitrarily executed, lightning-fast alternations, by lightly taking out and taking in the nose according to momentary need, to promote the elastically from-behind-to-front swinging back muscles in this oscillation, to tension them more in the forward direction (contact), or, in the case of excessive swing, by lightly hollowing action through taking out the nose, to send a counter-wave, so to speak, against it, in order to check it lightly and in good time, not allowing it to swing fully forward.

And likewise conversely! The hindquarters are to lead in lifting the forehand from the ground: a slight taking out of the nose releases the tension in front; the hindquarters, supporting themselves on the ground, increase their tension and draw the forehand playfully toward themselves,[88] whereas sharper contact at this moment makes the lifting more difficult or regulates it by exerting a forward pull on the hindquarters.

Herein also lies the quite natural explanation of why Fillis always wants the nose somewhat in front of the vertical. He rides only lessons in which the hindquarters have to draw the forehand to themselves, to take it toward themselves; thus he can only use the pull in this direction. It would, however, be entirely erroneous to assume that Fillis therefore never allows the swing to be released forward. On the contrary, at the moment of stepping or, more correctly, arching- or hollowing-moment, the direction of the pull changes. Whereas there the pull is a very powerful one, here it is restricted to a small degree, so that it only brings about the "letting go of the jaw" (contact without any sinking of the neck).

Fillis himself illustrates this in the striking example of the balloon of swing released by the hindquarters and the little string that the hand yields (remark on page 166 of his work).

We campaign riders, too, use in dressage almost exclusively the pull in the direction: "hindquarters take the forehand to themselves." This lies quite simply in the innate tendency of the horse to go more burdened in front. We truly do not need to encourage this artificially.

This does not, however, by any means imply that riding in equally or even approximately equally high neck- and head-position is the true thing for us. As

---

[88] *This interplay of musculature can be illustrated by a very simple example. One imagines on a small board, at suitable distances, two small gallows, one representing the croup, the other the withers of the horse, and a third, higher one, representing the weight. Over croup and weight, but under the withers, one runs a rubber band, nails it firmly behind the croup, grasps it in front of the weight with the hand and tensions it fairly tightly. If one now lets go, the fixed end immediately pulls the end in the hand toward itself. If one tensions the hand again, the pull becomes reciprocal. If one tensions even more sharply, one will finally, given sufficient strength of the rubber band, lift the end of the board on which the end of the rubber band marking the hind legs is nailed. The force of existing tension, when released at one end, will always pull the other toward itself. These effects and counter-effects have already been discussed in analogous fashion in the first chapter; the explanations there and here supplement one another.*

Natural Horsemanship

we have already explained elsewhere in this chapter, the different purpose for which Fillis and *Natural Horsemanship* consistently think, with the same natural necessity with which we seek to build all relations between rider and horse, compels him to his entirely high, us to lower neck- and head-positions. And further, we have just demonstrated that not the high position, but the possibility, in case of need, to take the nose out to a measured degree and nevertheless, a tenth of a second later, to act with contact, without again obtaining too much downward swing, is what is significant about the handling under discussion.

In a word, therefore, as the footnote on page 21 already expressed it: we take in dressage the nose lightly in front of the vertical whenever too much swing or too much tension of the back muscles confronts us disturbingly in the work. We allow contact where this is not detrimental. And we consider the greatest possible promotion of contact itself through firm resistance of the hand, provided the horse remains in balance, to be entirely appropriate where a weak back or a horse holding back allows too little forward swing. Where one rides well driven, there is, of course, never any lack of contact.

Otherwise, as in chapter four on collection has already explained, we allow every horse to seek for itself that assembly of its body which suits it best as an individual; we merely ensure, through thorough loosening of jaw and back, that it can also assume the position most favorable to its individuality (see page 98 ff.). Complaints about lack of depth of position will never be raised here by adherents of *Natural Horsemanship*, as the Wochenblatt article of 1900 proves irrefutably. It will, however, occur that with more difficult horses we do not fully permit contact itself in use, in the interest of balance.[89]

But in yet another respect, the Fillis handling, so long as one does not divide the reins, contains a quite remarkable peculiarity of effect. I have already mentioned in chapter six the thoroughbred mare on which I made my first experiences with the Fillis handling. She canters for herself and the rider most pleasantly with a lightly elevated neck and a lightly forward-placed nose. Any deep contact causes her, in fast canter, to lose balance. In the described position, which she assumes of her own accord, she is, despite her extremely favorable conformation, thoroughly soft and comfortable.

This chapter already mentioned how striking it is that this most sensitive rider of all times has nothing to say about crookedness except for occasional mention of the fact. One reason for this, namely that it becomes almost imperceptible with lightly relaxed upper muscles (= forward-placed nose), I already indicated there. The second lies in the thorough working of the jaw from the hand. The third, however, lies in the peculiarity of the Fillis handling now under discussion!

---

[89] *The above-mentioned thoroughbred mare, on which I made my first experiences with the Fillis handling, canters for rider and horse most pleasantly with a lightly elevated neck and lightly forward-placed nose. Any deep contact causes her, in fast canter, to lose balance. In the described position, which she assumes of her own accord, she is, despite her extremely favorable conformation, entirely soft and comfortable.*

The snaffle reins are namely not divided, but are drawn fully through the hand and thus stand so that they act evenly on the bars. Now, the crooked horse regulates for itself the bilateral length, and quite of its own accord one rein becomes a little longer, the other shorter. Since Fillis uses the curb reins, which tension the upper muscles, only when he has the hind legs thoroughly under himself, he will up to this moment, because of the advanced nose and the relaxed upper muscles, scarcely notice anything of the crookedness. Since, on the other hand, good stepping-under of the hindquarters immediately produces pushing-off and yielding at the jaw, the crookedness also appears only slightly disturbing to him when using the curb reins, especially since his play of fingers maintains an uninterrupted alternation between the snaffle effect that eliminates crookedness and the curb effect that provokes it. I myself make this experience every time I ride with Fillis handling,[90] I would, however, like to add that with her as well, the work is essentially accelerated through the use of crookedness. In particular, the first travers-like hollow bending of the difficult side is very quickly achieved through rapidly successive light bringing-in on the favorable side, combined with vigorous turning through on the unfavorable side using the curb reins (with the bradoon alone, the lower reins).

That with Fillis too the mane crest changes sides according to the bend (a sign of correct hollow bending) is clearly shown by the photogravures, especially on Plate XXXV, Figures 1 and 2, Plates XXXII and XXXI. In Figure 2, the moment when the mane is in the process of passing from one side to the other stands out very clearly, and on Plate XXV (Germinal in right and left counter-canter) it is already correctly placed, i.e., in Figure 2 to the right, in Figure 1 to the left.

The complete straightening that this signifies is achieved by Fillis, in my conviction, primarily through the continued changing of the canter, on which he places an extraordinarily strong emphasis. This is also of great interest for our purposes: a frequent change in canter—more precisely, such frequent practice of that canter which the horse is at the moment less inclined to strike off on (the side changes because crookedness, as we saw in chapters five and six, also continually changes)—until the horse willingly and securely strikes off equally on both hands, is a purely practical means of eliminating crookedness. It must only be observed that the horse is sharply set between straightening aids in the process, and does not arbitrarily deviate from the straight line with a hind leg.

---

[90] *I do this only exceptionally, in order to remain in constant close contact with the way in which the "ordinary man" rides. Besides, one can also, with our handling, once one has grasped the meaning of the Fillis handling, produce analogous effects; only an extremely rapid yet infinitely soft raising and lowering of the hand is required for this.*

Conclusion

In conclusion, a brief word about the form in which *Natural Horsemanship* appears before the public.

That author and publisher are, in reality, not separate personalities will scarcely have escaped the knowledgeable reader.

Various circumstances led to this separation.

The first five chapters were written in the period from 1885 to about 1891. They then lay dormant until the end of 1900, when the decision to publish matured.

The necessity of altering certain things was present. But for me personally, everything was so firmly interlocked that I did not feel capable of making changes in the text itself. Thus I helped myself by means of the concluding words and annotations of the publisher.

Moreover, this offered the advantage of being able partly to point out especially important points, and partly—where the text of the "author" presented objections that naturally arose from the conclusions meanwhile reached—to refute these in advance "as publisher."

A revision was excluded for yet another reason.

The first five chapters truly appeared to me as though written by a stranger when I took them out of the desk after so long a time. As repeatedly indicated, a so-to-speak modern study of the art of riding, as it would present itself to me from my present standpoint, is conceivable only after the creation of entirely new terms that fully correspond to the matters they designate.

With concepts such as "upright carriage," "on the bit," "standing on the rein," etc., one can only work with endless circumlocutions in order ultimately to produce nothing but misunderstanding and confusion. The history of riding theory has thus far been nothing more than a continued chain of misunderstandings! (Cf. Introduction of the "Militär-Wochenblatt" article of 1892 on page 202.)

A sudden detachment from those concepts—originating in the old high school and, in my view, obsolete—would, however, have interrupted the connection with the reader in an even more unfortunate manner.

Thus I had to content myself with the attempt to demonstrate that every function of the forehand, by its inner nature, is for the rider merely a value factor dependent on the activity of the hindquarters and the back, i.e., something entirely indifferent both for an irreproachable theory and for practical dressage.

Only when the equestrian atmosphere has absorbed such conceptions to the point of saturation is the ground prepared for "new values."

Only these will ensure conciseness and clarity for the theoretical system, and simplicity and general comprehensibility for the practical method.

Appendix A

Source: *"Militär-Wochenblatt,"* Nr. 65, 7. August 1886

Are Modifications in the Training of the Soldier's Horse Necessitated by the Increased Demands Placed upon the Cavalry?

By
Paul Plinzner,
First Lieutenant of the Landwehr Cavalry,
Stable Master to His Royal Highness Prince Wilhelm of Prussia.

Under the altered tactical conditions which have arisen from the enormous development of firearms, there is within our cavalry a lively striving and struggle to maintain itself at the level of the current situation and to assert a justified position alongside the other branches of arms.

If this earnest striving must arouse interest and attention in everyone who stands in any kind of relationship to the cavalry, then this is so in an even higher degree for that person for whom, from youth onward, the horse has been the embodiment of all that is beautiful. This is especially true of one who, for a longer series of years, has lived professionally, with undivided zeal, solely for the art of riding, in theory and in practice, as is the case with the writer of these lines.

May the gentlemen professional cavalrymen therefore take my lively interest in the arm in good part. In what follows, I submit for their consideration a few thoughts on that area of cavalry technique in which I can, at any rate, claim to possess a judgment—namely, the training of the horse.

If, in my exposition, I shall deviate to some extent from the principles generally prevailing, I nevertheless shall certainly not permit myself to propose anything which I have not long and thoroughly tested in practice and found confirmed by success.

I do not flatter myself with expecting to find general approval, but am fully prepared for contradiction. Nevertheless, I still hope to find, in some like-minded souls, understanding and assent.

It is undisputed that the cavalry can only be relied upon for effective intervention in battle if it is capable of covering long distances at great speed. That is, it must ride at a very extended gallop without losing the posture, composure, and energy required for the attack. Accordingly, and with full justification, the emphasis of the entire cavalry training lies in the so-called galloping of squadrons. The indispensable requirements in this respect are therefore sought essentially through a certain habituation of work.

Although I am far from declaring this habituation work superfluous, nevertheless, I believe that it could be made much easier. I also believe that performance could be further increased if greater attention were already paid, in the training of the horses, to bringing them into those forms which are the most practical for the demands placed upon them. No one will dispute that the ideal cavalry horse of today is the one that gallops like a good hunting horse. At the same time, it must possess that collection which is just as indispensable for riding in ranks and files as it is for individual combat.

If we now observe the squadrons when riding at extended pace, we shall have to admit that, in general, the first requirement is not met. The good hunting horse gallops with a low nose and an arched back; the great majority of squadron horses, on the other hand, gallop with a high nose and a hollowed back. As a result of this, the hunting horse moves in long, calm bounds with relatively little expenditure of strength, while the squadron horse generally moves in shorter, less enduring bounds with relatively much greater expenditure of strength.

If one now objects that this has its cause in the unskillfulness of the riders, then I am far from underestimating the difficulties resulting from the latter. Nevertheless, I believe that, since the cavalry is in the favorable position of being able to keep its horses raw and unspoiled and to proceed slowly in their training, it ought to be possible to achieve that the majority of the horses gallop with a low nose, without thereby falling short of the necessary requirements of collection.

That this is generally not achieved has its reason in the fact that with "uprighting" and "bringing into the bridle," the two great factors of training, proper economy is not practiced. Instead, almost everywhere the former is pursued at the expense of the latter in the working of the horses. The great majority of cavalry riding masters still stand de facto at the point of view of seeing the quintessence of training in uprighting, without sufficiently considering that the latter, by its very nature, may only advance to the degree that the hind legs learn to bend and spring under the load, and that "uprighting" can only be of use when it is paired with unconditional acceptance of the bridle,[91] because only the latter guarantees the passing through of the aids.

By no means do I deny that the initial riding-in of young horses is handled throughout the cavalry in a very competent manner, in that they are brought to the point of seeking the reins with a low nose in a certain "direction toward the shoulders."[92] I do, however, find that on average this indispensable

---

[91] *I call acceptance of the bridle unconditional when the horse gives way to every resistance with neck and head against the hand, regardless of whether the rider gives up the hand or not. An acceptance of the bridle in which the horse is forcibly held, whether with or without auxiliary reins, is not unconditional.*

[92] *"Direction toward the shoulders," "direction into balance," "direction on the haunches." These designations, which explain themselves, are found in Louis Seeger's* System of the Art of Riding *and Gustav Steinbrecht's* Gymnasium of the Horse [Xenophon Press], *the latter title having been edited by the author of the present article.*

Appendix A

foundation is not only insufficiently consolidated, but is, as a rule, even more or less shaken as soon as the actual working of the horses begins, which aims at collection.

When one strives to bring the gaits as far as possible into the normal posture with the poll as the highest point of the forehand, the uprighting work begins. In doing so, one may endeavor to drive the hind feet well under the mass. Nevertheless, the correct relationship between this driving-under of the hindquarters and the uprighting of the forehand is so difficult to achieve that the horse is only rarely maintained, in such work, in unconditional acceptance of the bridle. As a rule, this is very soon more or less lost, and with that, the disturbance of the foundation has already occurred.

If this defect is recognized immediately, the collecting work is stopped at once and one returns to the "direction toward the shoulders," in free gaits, first to bring about again the loosening of the poll. In this way the damage that has already occurred to the foundation can still be repaired. If, however—and this happens in by far the majority of cases—one continues instead, forcing the horse, under increased loading of the back, by sitting into the stiff poll, in the hope that the forehand will in time settle itself of its own accord, then the verdict is pronounced upon the horse, and the stamp of the [Schenkelgänger] "leg-movers."[93] with all its disadvantages for this life is impressed upon it.

---

[93] *Stable Master v. Holleuffer, in his work on pillar work, distinguishes between (Schenkelgänger) "leg-movers" [hind-leg evader] and (Rückengänger) "back-movers" [back-engaged] horses. Horses which, in movement, form an elastic, spring-like connection between forehand and hindquarters through a certain [positive] tension of the back muscles—brought about by the arching of the back—so that the gait itself also becomes springy, he calls "back-movers." On the other hand, those horses in which this elasticity of the connection, and thus also of the gait, is lacking—because the back is either hollowed or held rigidly and spasmodically—he calls "leg-movers.") -* **Plinzner footnote.**

Translator's note: Schenkelgänger *("leg-movers" or better said "hind-leg evader")*
The German term **Schenkelgänger** *designates a horse that avoids true engagement by stepping laterally with the hind leg(s) rather than stepping forward and under the body to carry weight. Instead of bending the joints of the hindquarters and accepting load, the horse shifts the hind leg sideways, thereby evading the gymnastic demands of collection. This false activity is often accompanied by stiffness of the back and neck and is frequently produced by premature or forced attempts at collection, excessive lateral work, or reliance on the hand to create a false, premature elevated posture. Classical German authors consistently condemn the Schenkelgänger as a deceptive form of obedience: the horse appears compliant and active, yet avoids the essential work of weight-bearing behind.*

Translator's note: Rückengänger *("back-movers" or "back-engaged horses")*
The German term Rückengänger denotes a horse that moves through an elastic, lifted back, transmitting the propulsive and carrying forces of the hindquarters correctly through the body. In such a horse, the hind legs step forward and under the mass, the joints of the haunches bend to accept load, and the back forms a supple, weight-bearing bridge between hindquarters and forehand. The gaits are consequently elastic, balanced, and enduring. In classical German riding theory, the Rückengänger represents the properly trained horse—capable of sustained work, genuine collection, and long-term soundness—whether in cavalry service or in advanced school riding.

The longer one sins against the animal in this manner, the more the elasticity of the back, and thereby of the gait, is suppressed, the more it becomes a habit for the horse to brace itself against the rider with a stiff poll. We must not conceal from ourselves that in the majority of cases this is the course of events, and that the majority of our squadron horses are "leg-movers."

If we consider the natural gaits of our horses, then unless we wish to indulge in fundamental illusions, we must admit that it will be impossible with many of them to bring them into the normal form. This is simply because the dimensions required for this are not present—quite apart from the influences of the back and the forehand—such that we shall be forced to make concessions either with regard to "acceptance of the bridle" or to "uprighting." At this point we arrive at the focal point of our discussion.

It cannot for a moment be doubtful, if we make it clear to ourselves, that we have an unconditional need for acceptance of the bridle, and that all uprighting without acceptance of the bridle not only avails us nothing, but on the contrary does us [and the horses] direct harm.

In the long run, a horse is only capable of uniform, powerful, and elastic movements under the load of the rider if it has brought its back into a certain arching and thereby its back muscles into a certain [positive] tension, so that as Stable Master von Holleuffer aptly calls them the "oscillations" of the back become possible. These oscillations, in turn, impart the springing quality to the gait and as the same author says, "play into the hand with unconditional obedience."

This arching of the back, or tension of its muscles, through which a firm, elastic, springing connection between forehand and hindquarters is established, we achieve naturally through acceptance of the bridle. Within this limit, achieved through acceptance of the bridle by the activity of the hindquarters, a horse that goes with a high nose and stiff poll is brought to yielding, that is, induced through acceptance of the bridle to arch the back.

Anyone who has perceived and confirmed in himself the striking difference in feeling this success before and after will understand what is meant by a "back-mover" and what by a "leg mover." Whoever has ever had this feeling will agree with me not only that, in training, every step taken without acceptance of the bridle is a mistake, but also that it is an irresponsible waste of the strength of rider and horse to demand performance from the latter without having it in acceptance of the bridle.

Since every hunting rider is clear on this point, that he can only ride with pleasure and success on a galloping horse that is in acceptance of the bridle, it seems to me that the cavalryman, under today's demands on his arm, is in exactly the same position. I would therefore like to establish the fundamental principle:

> Our first and most essential striving in the training of the cavalry horse must be to confirm it in unconditional acceptance of the bridle.

Appendix A

As far as the collection indispensable for the soldier's horse is concerned, we require for this the "direction into balance," which is known to be achieved only by transferring part of the weight of the forehand onto the hindquarters—in two ways: by driving the hind feet toward the center of gravity, and by uprighting the forehand.

Since, as we have seen, this work succeeds in the rarest cases without impairing the unconditional acceptance of the bridle, which is necessary to us in the first instance, it therefore becomes a matter of finding means and ways of avoiding this danger. I believe that the manner and method in which I have personally worked my horses with success for years may perhaps be the one that most simply solves this problem.

The matter is simply this: that in collecting work I fundamentally avoid all uprighting with the hand, i.e., I never make use of upward-directed pulls of the hand, but allow the hand to act only in a purely backward direction, that is, parallel to the spinal column.

Since I have secured unconditional acceptance of the bridle in young horses by riding forward in the "direction toward the shoulders," and in older ones, which have long been ridden with a stiff poll, by provoking yielding through the spur against the restraining hand, these purely backward restraining aids act by loading and thereby bending the hind legs, which I animate through light leg or spur aids.

The rein action of the hand and the simultaneous leg aids must thereby always meet the hind foot precisely when it is in the act of stepping forward, which is quite easy, because the horse gives these moments to the softly seated rider. When, in these moments, the approaching leg or spur stimulates the hind foot to further stepping forward, the restraint of the hand meets it during the moment of setting down, loading, and thereby bends it.

Naturally, backward action of the hand, in that they bring the nose closer to the chest, act to upwardly-direct and compress the neck, so that it emerges at the withers. They do not suppress the activity of the back and, on the contrary, promote it.

In this way, without working in an uprighting manner, I achieve the degree of raising the forehand [individually] appropriate to each horse, without endangering acceptance of the bridle and thereby the arching of the back. In this elevation, the horse then carries itself of its own accord, because it is based solely on the strength of the hindquarters.

Therefore, the result is that the fully trained horse worked in this manner raises itself in the forehand all the more as I continue to develop thrust [from the haunches] and the more deeply it settles behind. The more I allow the bending [of the haunches and the respective] force of the hindquarters to act, the more the horse raises its forehand respectively without my ever having to carry the weights of the forehand in the hand.

If I let my entire work be guided by this main principle, I serve myself primarily in order to train a hind leg in stronger articulation. Likewise, similar raising of the forehand is achieved in the bent lessons and the lateral movements however, I practice these only with a very limited degree of bending. With half shoulder-in and half counter-shoulder-in at the trot and in the canter, I generally manage perfectly and collect my horses to very collected canters. I am able to collect the trot all the way to passage, without making use of any special auxiliary aids, and with some horses, to a greater degree of collection to piaffe. This level of collection probably goes beyond the requirements of the cavalry. Nevertheless, I maintain in all bent lessons [relative] straightness, beginning with the lateral stepping of a hind leg. As long as I can keep the horse [functionally] straight, even in bending, I also have it in obedience.[94]

The essence of what I have said about my method of dressage is therefore this:

the collection of the horse occurs through the counteracting of the forces of the hindquarters on the one hand, and the weight of the forehand on the other.

The elevation of the forehand must be solely the result of collection and must not be sought through elevating work of the hand.

To the person who has rightly understood me and feels what I mean, I can promise from my own experience not only that you will always be cheerful and light-hearted in your work, because you will always have springs under yourself. Furthermore, on this finished horse ridden outdoors, one will be able to ride quickly with true pleasure, the lance in the left, the sabre in the right.

I have the moral conviction that if cavalry work were carried out according to these principles, the majority of its horses would be brought close to this ideal: they would gallop like hunting horses and yet possess the collection of the soldier's horse. I admit that they might, in part, perhaps go with very low noses—this reproach is often made against my horses as well—but they would all be "back-movers." Moving in this way they would not only be far more under the control of their riders, but would also preserve themselves far better than the [artificially] uprighted horse.

The horse that goes with a high nose and stiff poll is not only the one that stumbles most easily, but also the one that most quickly ruins its legs. The galloping performance of the squadrons, and thereby the prospect of successful cavalry intervention in battle, could certainly be increased considerably if on such a training foundation, the same care were applied to

---

[94] *Even General von Schmidt, in his "Instructions," published by Riding Master von Bockelberg, emphasizes how the obedience of the horse essentially depends upon its straightness. Indeed, I should like to indulge the hope that the General would have found my views on cavalry horse dressage somewhat worthy of consideration.*

habituation work and training—if I may call it that—as is done now, without the handiness of the horses suffering in the least.

In conclusion, I would like to preemptively address two objections that have more than once been raised against me in oral discussions on this subject.

The *first* is that, with my method of approaching the collecting work, horses easily come behind the bridle. I maintain, however, that anyone to whom this happens understands very little about utilizing the strength of the hindquarters. However, whoever works his horse in collected and energetic gaits is safeguarded against this danger under all circumstances.

The *second* objection is that such work could only be carried out by very skillful people. I cannot refrain from replying that upright seat and firm lateral positions, in order to remain even and harmless, require far greater skill.

I must set one condition: namely, that before we seat the recruits on the horses to be trained, we teach our them a soft, supple seat—which is also by no means anything particularly difficult, since the peasant lad, who sits with dangling legs riding bare back on his horse, has this soft seat as long as he does not stiffen himself in anticipation of any danger.

However, if instead of allowing the gracefulness of form to develop incidentally of itself, we begin by pressing the recruit from the outset into the mold of the military seat, then we cannot be surprised if he never acquires the feeling for the movements of the horse.

The decisive factor in working the horse with this soft seat is that the effects of hand and leg always strike the horse at the correct moments, which I have described more closely above. The naturally seated rider is given these moments by the horse. Conversely, the rider who stiffens himself misses these feelings and never applies his aids at the right time.

Therefore the soft, supple seat is the foundation of all correct horse training.

It has long been my wish to present a brief outline of my principles on cavalry training. Based on my personal experience and my observations on the riding and exercise grounds, I consider them well suited to keeping the army in full accordance with today's demands and in a contemporary manner.

In presenting these views, I am prepared for much disapproval, but hope just as firmly for the sympathy of some kindred soul.

Publisher's Afterword

Readers often arrive at the end of this book with a question that seems unavoidable: *Who, finally, is right?* Is it Fillis, with his brilliance and commanding hand? Is it Plinzner, with his insistence on hindquarter engagement and work from back to front? Or is it the author himself, who has guided us patiently through page after page of analysis, only to step forward at the end and reveal his own hand behind the curtain?

The answer, if one has truly followed the argument of the book, is that *the question itself dissolves.*

This work does not exist to declare a victor in a contest of names. Indeed, one of its most consistent warnings is directed precisely against that habit of thought—the tendency to replace understanding with allegiance, to substitute banners for reasoning. The very phrases that once animated the riding world—the *Fillis followers, the Plinzners*—are shown here to be symptoms of a deeper error: the belief that truth in horsemanship can be inherited by association rather than earned through causality.

Fillis is not dismissed. His accomplishments remain undeniable, his refinement admirable. But the book demonstrates, quietly and relentlessly, that brilliance of result does not suffice as proof of correctness in principle. A method that depends on exceptional talent, exceptional horses, and exceptional hands cannot serve as a general foundation. Where Fillis begins with the forehand and seeks posture first, the author asks a more fundamental question: *What must occur in the horse's body for such posture to arise without contradiction?* When examined under that light, the Fillis method proves visually persuasive but causally incomplete.

Plinzner, by contrast, emerges far closer to the natural order. His insistence that collection must arise from behind, that the back must transmit the work of the hindquarters forward, and that the forehand can only be shaped as a consequence rather than a cause, is repeatedly confirmed by anatomy, balance, and experience. Yet even here, the book refuses to allow a coronation. Plinzner's ideas are validated—but Plinzner the authority is deliberately set aside. The reader is never asked to believe him because he is Plinzner, but only insofar as his conclusions survive scrutiny.

And finally, the author himself steps into view—not to claim victory, but to make it impossible. By revealing that editor, author, and publisher of the 1905 German edition, are one and the same, he removes the last refuge of borrowed authority. No external prestige remains. No appeal to reputation is left standing. What remains is only the argument itself.

In this sense, the book has no winner in the conventional meaning of the word. Or rather, it has only one: *natural law.*

Again and again, the author returns to the same uncompromising test. What follows necessarily from balance? What follows from anatomy? What follows when the horse is allowed—and required—to organize itself without coercion? Each time, the answer points in the same direction: from back to front, from cause to effect, from engagement to posture, from balance to expression.

If there is a quiet triumph here, it belongs not to a man or a method, but to a way of thinking. A way that refuses shortcuts. A way that distrusts appearances. A way that asks not *what looks correct, but what must be correct*.

That this debate still feels contemporary more than a century later is no accident. The tension between appearance and substance, between hand and seat, between imposed form and earned balance, has never been fully resolved—only renamed. This book reminds us that the resolution has always been available to those willing to follow the chain of cause and effect all the way back to its origin.

In the end, the author leaves us with no doctrine to memorize, no school to join, no name to invoke. He leaves us instead with a discipline of thought—and with the horse, quietly returning the verdict through its body, its balance, and its willingness.

Richard F. Williams
Translator/Publisher

Xenophon Press Library
www.XenophonPress.com
Xenophon Press is dedicated
to preserving classic equestrian literature.
We publish both new and historic works, and original translations.

30 Years with Master Nuno Oliveira, Henriquet 2011

A Journey Through the Horse's Body, Fritz 2012

A Rider's Survival from Tyranny, de Kunffy 2012

A Voice for the Horse, Saint Ryan 2025

Another Horsemanship, Racinet 1994

Academic Art of Riding, Bent Branderup 2024

Austrian Art of Riding, Poscharnigg 2015

Broken or Beautiful: The Struggle of Modern Dressage, Barbier/Conrod 2020

Classic Show Jumping: the de Nemethy Method, de Nemethy 2016

Classical Dressage with Anja Beran, Beran 2021

Collection or Contortion: Anatomy and Biomechanics of Positioning and Bend, Gerd Heuschmann, 2024

Divide and Conquer Book 1, Lemaire de Ruffieu 2016

Divide and Conquer Book 2, Lemaire de Ruffieu 2017

Dressage for the 21st Century, Belasik 2001

Dressage in the French Tradition, Diogo de Bragança 2011

Dressage Principles and Techniques: A Blueprint for the Serious Rider, Tavora 2018

Dressage Principles Illuminated, Expanded Edition, de Kunffy 2021

École de Cavalerie Part II, Expanded Edition, Robichon de la Guérinière 2015

Elements of Dressage, von Ziegner 2022

Enlightened Horsemanship in 18th-Century Britain, Alison Moller 2026

Equestrian Art: The Collected Early Writings (1951-1956), Nuno Oliveira 2022

Equestrian Art: The Collected Later Works, Nuno Oliveira 2022

Equine Osteopathy: What the Horses Have Told Me, Giniaux 2014

Federico Grisone's "The Rules of Riding," Grisone/Tobey 2023

Fragments from the Writings of Max Ritter von Weyrother, Fane 2017

François Baucher: The Man and His Method, Baucher/Nelson 2013

French Equitation: a Baucherist in America, 1922
    & Hand-book for Horsewomen, Bussigny 2023

General Chamberlin: America's Equestrian Genius, Matha 2020

Great Horsewomen of the 19th Century in the Circus, Nelson 2015

Gymnastic Exercises for Horses Volume II, Eleanor Russell 2013

H. Dv. 12 with Commentary: The Rulebook of Riding Culture,
    Heuschman/von Ziegner/Williams 2024

Handbook of Jumping Essentials, Lemaire de Ruffieu 2015

Handbook of Riding Essentials, Lemaire de Ruffieu 2015

Healing Hands: Equine Acupressure and First Aid, Giniaux, DVM 1998

Horse Training: Outdoors and High School, Beudant 2014

Horsemanship & Horsemastership Volume 1, US Cavalry 2021

Horsemanship Training Films 3 DVD set, US Cavalry 2021

I, Siglavy, Asay 2018

Learning to Ride, Santini 2016

Legacy of Master Nuno Oliveira, Millham 2013

Lessons in Lightness: Expanded Edition, Mark Russell 2019

Mark of Clover, Barczy Kelly, 2022

Methodical Dressage of the Riding Horse, Faverot de Kerbrech 2010

Mein Pferd hat die Nase vorn!, Heuschmann 2025

Military Equitation or, A Method of Breaking Horses, and Teaching Soldiers to
    Ride, Pembroke, and *A Treatise on Military Equitation*, Tyndale 2018

My Horses Have Something to Say, de Wispelaere 2021

My Horse is in front of the Vertical!, Heuschmann/Williams 2025

Natural Horsemanship, Based on the papers of a passionate riding instructor,
    de la croix/Williams 2025

Précis D'Équitation, de Weck 2025

Principles of Dressage and Equitation, a.k.a. Breaking and Riding, Fillis 2017

Principles of Equitation A Swiss Cavalry Manual, de Weck/Williams 2026

Racinet Explains Baucher, Racinet 1997

Releasing the Jaw, Poll, and Neck DVD, Mark Russell 2021

Riding and Schooling Horses, Chamberlin 2020

Riding by Torchlight, Cord 2019

Riding in Rhyme, Davies 2021

Seat, Gaits & Reactions, de Sévy, 2023

Schooling Exercises In-Hand, Hilberger 2009

Science and Art of Riding in Lightness, Stodulka 2015

Shoulder-in: Secret of the Art of Equitation, Salins/Williams 2025

Sketches of the Equestrian Art, Barbier/Sauvat 2022

The Art of Ridin Odin at Saumur, Philippe Karl 2024

The Art of Riding a Horse, D'Eisenberg 2015

The Art of Traditional Dressage, Volume 1 DVD, de Kunffy 2013

The Chamberlin Reader, Chamberlin/Matha, 2020

The de Nemethy Method: A training seminar, 8 DVD set, de Nemethy 2019

The Essentials of Captain Charles Raabe's Method of High School Dressage, Decarpentry/Williams 2025

The Ethics and Passions of Dressage Expanded Edition, de Kunffy 2013

The Forward Impulse, Santini 2016

The Gymnasium of the Horse, Steinbrecht 2018

The Horses, a novel, Walker 2015

The Italian Tradition of Equestrian Art, Tomassini 2014

The Maneige Royal, de Pluvinel 2010, 2015

The New Method of Dressing Horses a.k.a. A General System of Horsemanship, Cavendish 2020

The Portuguese School of Equestrian Art, de Oliveira/da Costa 2012

The Pure Teachings of Classical Horsemanship, von Neindorff/Simms 2025

The Quest for Lightness in Equitation and Equestrian Questions, Nelson/L'Hotte 2021

The Rider forms the Horse, Udo Bürger & Otto Zietzschmann, 2024

The Spanish Riding School & Piaffe and Passage, Decarpentry 2013

The Spanish Riding School: The Miracle of the White Horse DVD, US Lipizzan Association 2021

To Amaze the People with Pleasure and Delight, Walker 2015

Total Horsemanship, Racinet 1999

Training Hunters, Jumpers, and Hacks, Chamberlin 2019

Training The Flying Changes, Thomas & Shana Ritter 2025

Training with Master Nuno Oliveira, 2 DVD set, Eleanor Russell 2016

Training Your Foal, Ettl 2022

Treasury of Primary Directives for the Equestrian Art, 1720 and Directives, 1898 for the Spanish Riding School of Vienna, Regenthal/Fane, Holbein-Holbeinsberg/Meixner/Williams 2025

Truth in the Teaching of Master Nuno Oliveira, Eleanor Russell 2015
Wisdom of Master Nuno Oliveira, de Coux 2012

www.ingramcontent.com/pod-product-compliance
Lightning Source LLC
Chambersburg PA
CBHW080501240426
43673CB00006B/253